The Deception of Religion

Discovering the difference between religion and relationship

by David Wlazlak

ISBN: 978-0-6151-9829-3

Author can be contacted at RomansTenMinistries@cox.net

Book design by Lienzos Graphics: eric@lienzosgraphics.com

Dedication

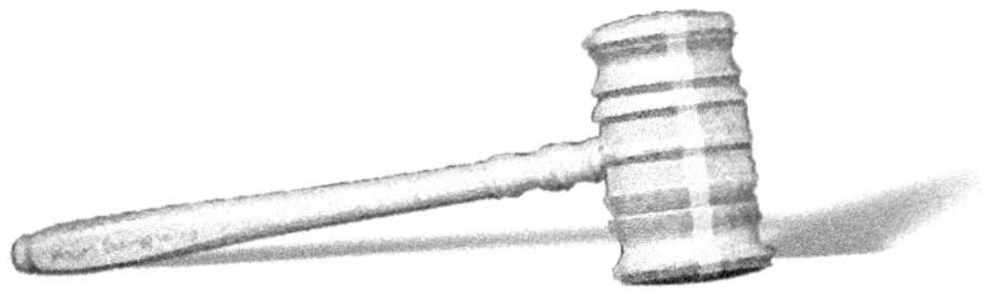

The "Deception of Religion" is dedicated to Henry E. Shaffer and Reverend Virgil L. Stokes. Without their faithful prayers, friendship, and impartation of the Word of God in my life this book would not have been written. I hope this book is a work they will be proud of. (Romans 1:11)

David P. Wlazlak

Table of Contents

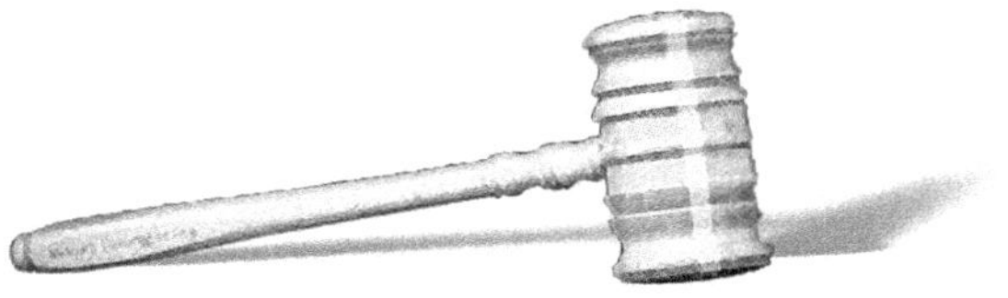

Acknowledgements

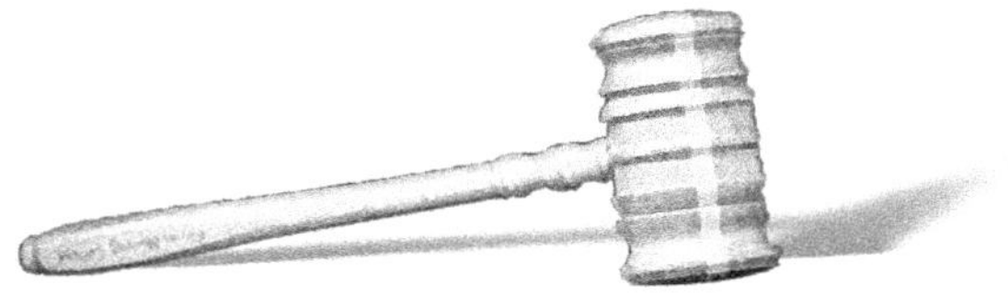

Thankful recognition is expressed to all those at "Faith Christian Fellowship Tucson" who have labored with me in the creation of "The Deception of Religion."

Each ones' love for me and the lost was manifested in the time all of you have spent assisting in the various details of its completion. (1 Corinthians 12:12-31) Special thanks to my wife, Kristie, for your heartfelt understanding of support during this assignment. (Proverbs 31)

Love

David P. Wlazlak

Foreword

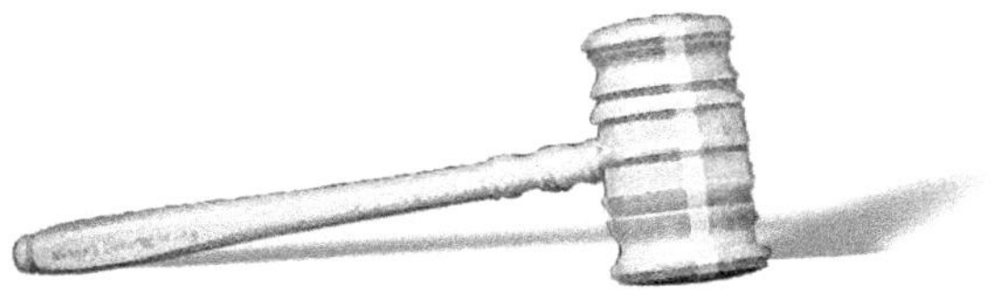

THE DECEPTION OF RELIGION

By David P. Wlazlak

The word of God with the refining fire of the Holy Spirit instructs all born again believers in Jesus Christ. The members of the one in three and three in one of the Holy Trinity are adamant in their objective of ensuring the protection of the Saints. The love Jesus Christ has for His Church was manifested on the Cross of Calvary, in the sending of the Holy Spirit, and continues to be manifested through the warnings they gave to the Church revealed through His word.

The reason that I wrote "The Deception of Religion" is to warn the universal body of Christ as to the purpose of Jesus Christ's disclosure of what will occur at "The Great White Throne Judgment," as it's called in the book of Revelation Chapter 20. The Holy Spirit compelled me to study the passage of scripture found in the gospel of Matthew, Chapter 7: 21-23—which, in my opinion, are the three most terrifying scriptures in the Bible! Until recently I was unqualified to teach others about this passage of scripture, but the Holy Spirit had been leading me to study and to ascertain the relevance of this portion of the dissertation given by Jesus Christ during His Sermon on the Mount. My previous attempts to try to understand this passage of scripture had always ended with many questions unanswered. The preservation of my soul had been the motivating factor in my perseverance in making peace with these scriptures. In the process of writing this book, I have discovered many truths that have brought me into a deeper personal relationship with God and that have assisted in liberating me from religious bondages.

The inspiration for this book was birthed in me in 2006. One desire in my heart was to warn the universal body of Christ of those who profess to be Christians but attempt to steal, kill, and destroy the sheep through religious deception. Many of these deceivers are presently attending Christian gatherings and believe they are on the path to Heaven. However, they have never been born again, and as a result their hearts are not right with God.

In addition, I wanted to ensure that this passage of scripture would no longer be used by church leadership to control the parishioners of their churches through fear and intimidation, and subjecting them to unnecessary religious regulations. This was not an enjoyable book to write, and will at times shake the very substance of people's foundations, but the awareness in my spirit reinforced my liability to properly represent the heart cry of the Holy Spirit and the will of God on this subject. Furthermore, I hope the readers will learn that God loves them more then words can express, and has given them clear instructions on how to truly know Him. I desire that all readers of this book will understand the importance and relevance of this prophetic utterance that was spoken by Jesus Christ.

> 21Not every one that saith unto me, Lord, Lord,
> shall enter into the kingdom of Heaven; but he
> that doeth the will of my Father which is in heaven.
> 22Many will say to me in that day, Lord, Lord, have
> we not prophesied in thy name? and in thy name
> have cast out devils? and in thy name done many
> wonderful works? 23And then will I profess unto
> them, I never knew you: depart from me, ye that
> work iniquity
>
> Matthew 7:21-23 (KJV)

Chapter One

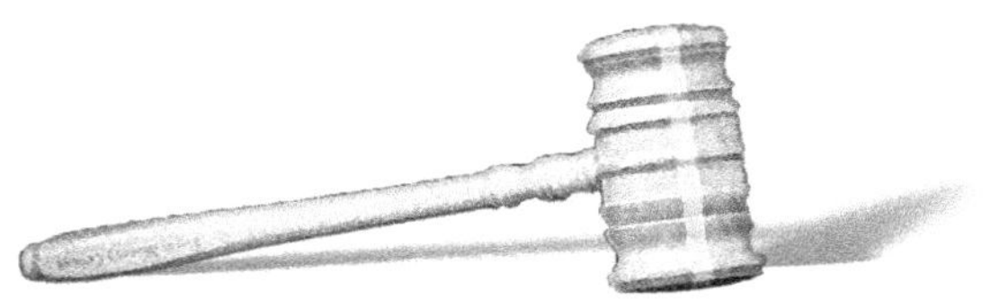

"Not every one that saith unto me, Lord, Lord, shall enter into the Kingdom of Heaven;..." (KJV)
Matthew 7:21

One day while I was meditating on the power of the confession one makes when becoming saved through Jesus Christ, my thoughts were interrupted by a co-worker. This co-worker had been compelled to use the name of Jesus Christ in a profane manner as he referred to the curvaceous backside of a female that had passed by him. I was immediately reminded that it was not just by acknowledging the Name of Jesus Christ that an individual becomes saved, but through accepting Jesus Christ as personal Lord and Savior.

One day while evangelizing with a brother in Jesus Christ I encountered a man and began to explain to him the simplicity of becoming born again. This man was open to the gospel and after telling him about Jesus, I led him in a prayer of repentance and verbal profession that Jesus Christ is his Lord and Savior. I commenced to tell the man that he was guaranteed a place in Heaven; however I did not explain to him the importance of believing what he had professed. Shortly afterwards, I was admonished by my Christian brother, and He instructed me to disclose the significance of what true repentance and confession in Jesus Christ means when someone accepts Him as his Savior. The word "repentance" is derived from the Greek word Mantaneo. In addition to meaning repentance, this Greek word carries the meaning of someone changing their mind, purposes and behavior. The conscious decision of an individual to change his thinking and behavior is a requirement of true repentance. Many professed Christians have not truly repented and as a result, they are still in their sins. The Apostle Peter understood that repentance was a prerequisite of salvation. In 2nd Peter 3:9, Peter proclaimed that God's will was that all would accept Jesus Christ and turn from their sins.

> "The Lord is not slack concerning His promise, as some count slackness, but is longsuffering toward us, not willing that any should perish but that all should come to repentance."
>
> 2 Peter 3:9

Having a remorseful heart before God is necessary before true conversion and the born again inwardness can occur in the spirit of a man. *Isaiah 29:13 "Therefore the Lord said: "Inasmuch as these people draw near with their mouths and honor Me with their lips, But have removed their hearts far from Me..."* I believe there are multitudes of professed Christians that have confessed belief in Jesus Christ but who have not repented. They may be in an unregenerate spiritual condition. True repentance first occurs in the mind and heart, and then confession is made unto salvation. After these changes occur the person is then regenerated by the Spirit of God. The regeneration provides the new birth which results in inheriting God's righteousness and true holiness. *Ephesians 4:22-24, "That you put off, concerning your former conduct, the old man which grows corrupt according to the deceitful lusts, and be renewed in the spirit of your mind, 24 and that you put on the new man which was created according to God, in true righteousness and holiness. (NKJV)*

Jesus rebuked many religious leaders by comparing them to trees that produced bad fruit because they had given credit to Satan for what Christ was doing through the assistance of the Holy Spirit. Jesus said, *"Out of the abundance of the heart the mouth speaks" (Matthew 12:34)* The legalistic Pharisees were furious that Jesus was healing the inflicted on the Sabbath day. They were uncompassionate towards the sick and deceived in their own self- righteousness. Their long awaited Messiah was standing before them and they were unable to recognize Him because they were blinded by the spirit of judgementalism. I believe this spirit contributed to concealing that Jesus Christ is the Sabbath. If they had known who was standing before them they could have ceased their unnecessary religious works and entered into rest. (Hebrews 4:10) Jesus said during His sermon on the mount in *Matthew 7:21, "Not everyone who says to Me, 'Lord,*

Lord,' shall enter the kingdom of heaven, but he who does the will of My Father in heaven." (The word for "Lord" in this passage of scripture is derived from the Greek word Kurios.) When Jesus used Kurios to describe Himself in this passage of scripture, He was calling Himself Elohim, which is one of the Hebrew names for God.

From a reading of the scriptures, it is apparent that there will be many people cast into the lake of fire who confessed that Jesus Christ was their Lord, who never truly repented. They will be brought before Him at the great white throne judgment and will be judged by their works. They will have knowingly refused to fulfill the requirements to be born again; however, they will proclaim that they had known Jesus Christ. When someone accepts the reconciliatory sacrifice of Jesus Christ, they will speak confession unto salvation (Matthew 12:34). It is quite possible for someone to make a profession of faith in Jesus Christ and not really believe that he is the "I AM." Jesus told the religious Jews that if they did not believe that he was the "I AM," they would die in their sins (John 8:24). There will be many that will confess, "Lord, Lord" at the great white throne judgment, and who will have believed that Jesus Christ existed, but will not have received Him as their God.

The Apostle Paul helped the Church in Rome to understand how to enter into a relationship with Christ, and also acquainted them with the spiritual principles that had already placed them "In Christ." When he wrote the passage of scripture in Romans 10:9-11, he was not only instructing them on how to lead people into salvation, but was telling them how their faith and commitment to Jesus Christ was manifested by their confessions. They were already saved before they received this epistle from Paul, but this epistle explained to them how the new birth had occurred within them: they had heard the word of God preached and believed in their hearts that Jesus Christ rose from the dead. (The Greek word for heart used in Romans 10:10 is Kardia and it describes the thoughts, desires, and true intentions of each individual.) Salvation occurs in the heart, and knowledge of the historicity of Jesus Christ's resurrection does not save a person. Each person must make a conscious decision to place Jesus Christ as Lord over his life. This commitment produces a cutting (Circumcision=cutting away of the sin nature) of the heart that allows the Holy Spirit into the spirit of man.

> "That if you confess with your mouth the Lord Jesus and believe in your heart that God has raised Him from the dead, you will be saved. For with the heart one believes unto righteousness, and with the mouth confession is made unto salvation."
>
> Romans 10:9-11

The word "confess" is derived from the Greek word Homologed. This Greek word carries the meaning of openly declaring a deep conviction. To give you some background, during the age of the early Church the Roman Emperors considered themselves avatars for Rome's pagan gods. Many of them considered themselves demigods, and it was customary for Roman citizens to worship them after their deaths as full-fledged gods. The penalty for giving allegiance to Jesus Christ as God was often death. The confessions made by many of the Saints of the early church were proclamations that cost them their very lives. Standing firm in their faith in the Deity, resurrection, and redemption of Jesus Christ resulted in diabolical persecution. What my early brothers and sisters in Christ endured to multiply the Church is astounding. The following shortlist shows the fates of some of Christianity's most famous adherents.

1. Stephen was stoned to death.
2. Matthias, who replaced Judas, was stoned and beheaded.
3. James' brother Jude was crucified.
4. Thomas was killed by a spear being lunged into him.
5. Luke was hung from an olive tree.
6. Paul was beheaded by Nero.
7. Peter was crucified upside down.

Why were they subjected to such barbaric treatment? It was for their confession in Jesus Christ. When Paul was writing to the Church in Rome the word "confess" carried with it the consequences of the members of that church being known as participants in the supposed heresy of the gospel. It meant that they had counted the cost of proclaiming their faith in Jesus Christ. They had decided that, regardless of the consequences, they would not deny Christ. These uncompromising mindsets were the cause of their persecution. This gives insight in the significance of the words spoken by Jesus recorded in the gospels of Matthew and Luke:

> "Therefore whoever confesses Me before men, him I will also confess before My Father who is in heaven. But whoever denies Me before men, him I will also deny before My Father who is in heaven."
>
> Matthew 10:32-33

> "And he who does not take his cross and follow after Me is not worthy of Me. He who finds his life will lose it, and he who loses his life for My sake will find it."
>
> Matt 10:38-39

> "Also I say to you, whoever confesses Me before men, him the Son of Man also will confess before the angels of God. But he who denies Me before men will be denied before the angels of God."
>
> Luke 12:8-9

A true confession of the saving grace of Jesus Christ should result in a desire to please God. There are Christians in the world today that are under terrible persecution. Most Christians living in the United States of America are sheltered from having to endure such persecution. The ministry that God calls members of the church into varies among individuals, and the proving of each individual's faith in Christ varies. However, God does have a job for every believer. Faith without works is dead, and good works should be a natural response to faith.

The Apostle Paul understood that a profession of faith in the message of salvation doesn't always mean that someone is saved. In the book of Acts there is a record of a woman with a demonic spirit who professed that Paul and his disciples were servants of the most High God. Furthermore, she proclaimed that they were showing the way of salvation. Paul was grieved in his spirit, and cast the demon out of her to shut her up (Acts 16:16-18). The message the demon was proclaiming through the woman was factually correct. However, her lifestyle was contradictory to the message Paul was preaching. Paul could not risk having people think that he agreed with her lifestyle simply because she had confessed the truth regarding his message of salvation. The objective of the demon was to water down the gospel by associating it with the religion of sorcery. Much like the sorceress, there are countless individuals who proclaim the gospel to be true, but whose lifestyles contradict the words that proceed from their mouths. Many of these people are involved in religious practices. However, they are tares planted by Satan. These tares are not a direct threat to the body of Christ. On the contrary, Jesus stated that they are to be left alone. In the parable of the tares and the wheat He warned of the damage it would cause to His church if they were removed, and said that the angels would remove them during harvest season on the last day. Attempting to remove them will cause damage to true believers and their families. Many tares attend church functions only to maintain peace with loved ones. If they were removed, it would cause undue hardships for the wheat. Tares proclaim faith in Jesus Christ but they do not really believe the gospel message and are not born of the Spirit of God. Despite all of this, the best place for them to be is in fellowship with believers. Many people have come to faith through the testimonies of their saved family members and associates. The job of judging the tares is reserved for Jesus Christ. Christians are called to love and pray for such people to come into a personal relationship with Jesus Christ. However, Christians should be aware of the worldly activities that the tares are involved in and distance themselves from their influence. It is not uncommon for tares to attend church activities for the sole purposes of peddling merchandise: this practice should be discouraged in a church setting, and reported to church leadership. Any time the tares start influencing the church to act in a worldly fashion, they need to be watched closely by church leadership.

Beware Of The Wolves

The Apostle Paul warned the Ephesian elders regarding wolves that would attempt to devour the sheep in his letter to them. These wolves need to be marked and removed from access to the sheep. This is the job of the Shepherd of the flock (the pastor). I believe that the following scriptures expose the characteristics of those who will be the recipients of those dreadful words, "I never knew you," that will be spoken by Jesus Christ at the great white throne judgment.

> 28Keep watch over yourselves and all the flock of
> which the Holy Spirit has made you overseers.
> Be shepherds of the church of God, which he
> bought with his own blood. 29I know that after
> I leave, savage wolves will come in among you
> and will not spare the flock. 30Even from your
> own number men will arise and distort the truth
> in order to draw away disciples after them. 31So
> be on your guard! Remember that for three years
> I never stopped warning each of you night and
> day with tears. 32"Now I commit you to God and
> to the word of his grace, which can build you up
> and give you an inheritance among all those who
> are sanctified.
>
> Acts 20:27-32 (NIV)

The Church is the property of Jesus Christ, and was purchased by His own blood. There are ravenous wolves that have entered into the universal body of Christ. They will want to be praised by others but do not really care about their admirers in the body. They will usually look just like the sheep they are planning to devour and will (on the surface) appear holy and pious. The Apostle Paul knew about wolves and warned the leaders through his letters that are contained in the New Testament. These wolves may have been believers in the gospel of Jesus Christ at one time; however, they departed from the faith under the influence of demonically inspired doctrines. It is essential to note that the passage of scripture found in Matthew 7:21-23 was spoken by Jesus after he warned of false prophets that would enter among the true believers. Please note: The passages of scripture previously listed are not referring to believers in Jesus Christ who have genuinely trusted in Him for their salvation. The warnings given by Paul and Jesus are for the shepherds to be on guard against wolves that come to scatter and devour the sheep. These wolves express that they know Jesus Christ, but their fruits reveal that they are drawing their inspiration from a lake of poisonous false doctrines. They have intentionally decided to become predators instead of protectors. Unfortunately, the fruits that expose these wolves don't manifest themselves immediately, and a church can be taken by surprise by them. These wolves will attempt to divide the flock by drawing sheep to themselves, and after they have accomplished their objective of drawing attention to themselves, they move on to the next flock. They are against authority and desire to make the shepherd look unqualified to care for the sheep. They do not care about the sheep and desire to cause division. They prey on the weaker sheep that are emotionally motivated. They will look for sheep that will listen to their doctrines and they will misquote what the shepherd says. These wolves do not care about applying the will of God to their lives, and are usually upset when attention is put on winning the lost for Christ. Wolves will preach doctrines that keep the saints in bondage to manmade religious rules and condemnation. These wolves are usually the reason churches split. They do not walk in love towards the brethren, and they reveal their "wolfish" characteristics by rebelling against church authority. When wolves accomplish their objective of division, the sheep are scattered, and many of them end up in the wilderness without a Shepherd. Without the protection from the Shepherd and his use of the Rod (the Word of God) they live a life of defeat. They have no one to properly groom them and assist them in carrying out the will of God for their lives. Pests will dig through the skins of the sheep and affect their mental stability. Their wool will become matted and easily ensnared. Their offspring will be born in danger of death from predators. In addition, scattered sheep are susceptible to disease and malnutrition. They will be tormented day and night outside the safety of the flock. Is it any wonder why there are so many warnings in the New Testament regarding wolves?

All Born Again People Know Jesus Christ

Having a born again conversion is a prerequisite to knowing Jesus Christ. Without the Holy Spirit taking up residence within the spirit of an individual he is incapable of understanding the will of God. Carrying out the will of God in his life is evidence that he has actually been born again. However, just because someone doesn't show a manifestation of the will of God in his life that does not mean he is not born again. He could be poorly taught and just simply carnal. Many people believe that Jesus Christ was crucified and was raised from the dead, but though they believe the facts of the Bible, they have little knowledge of how that relates to salvation. Even Satan and his fallen counterparts believe in Jesus Christ, but they are certainly not justified and righteous. It is necessary to commit one's life to Jesus Christ, realizing that redemption came with a price, and that that price was the sinless sacrifice of Jesus Christ on the cross of Calvary. When the blood of Jesus Christ dripped from His body down that old rugged cross it was buying back humanity from the slavery of sin, death, and religious rituals.

The power of the blood of Jesus contains within it the properties for the redemption of mankind. When the blood of Jesus Christ is applied to a repentant individual, it always produces a born again conversion which produces a new "spirit man." There should invariably be evidence of a desire to change sinful behavior, and express a life reflecting the glory of God. The Apostle Paul was changed instantly when he received Jesus as his Savior, and he began to work out his salvation from that moment forward. Following that episode the Holy Spirit then commenced to reveal what had occurred within him. The Apostle Paul explains the new birth to the Corinthian church in the following passage.

> "Therefore, if anyone is "In Christ," he is a new creation; old things have passed away; behold, all things have become new."
>
> 2 Corinthians 5:17

The term "In Christ" implies an inheritance of authority. If someone is "In Christ" he is standing in His aggregate identity. This term emphasizes the believer's authority to carry out the plans and will of Jesus Christ as His representative. I have worked in the law enforcement field for over thirteen years, and through my experiences as a law enforcement officer and a Christian, I've noticed that the authority that I have been given as a law enforcement officer is much like the authority I have "In Christ." In both the secular and spiritual realms I am accountable to higher powers. As a law enforcement officer, I am entrusted to enforce laws that have been established to ensure society is protected, and to ensure that the authorities above me are properly represented. With the given authorization to arrest and detain subjects that have violated the law of the land, the will of my superiors is expressed through my actions. Likewise, being given the authority of Jesus Christ as an ambassador for His will carries immeasurable amounts of responsibility.

When I became born again Jesus Christ gave me His legal authority to do the following: resist the Devil, enter into the throne room of God, and take authority over all the works of Satan. The main difference between the authority I have as a law enforcement officer compared to the authority given to me from Jesus Christ is that I never stop being in Christ. My life is in him now; I am his property and am commissioned to do his will. As a law enforcement officer my authority ceases when I am not under the scope of my employment. Throughout the tenure of my secular profession I have been disappointed by the lack of support that should have been rendered from the hierarchy I represented. It is encouraging to know that when I stand in the office of "Christian" I have the full support of the one I am representing. Jesus was rewarded for His obedience to the will of the Father. (Hebrews 1:4) When I became obedient to Jesus Christ by accepting his plan of redemption, I was birthed with His triumphant overcoming seed. This seed birthed within me contains the ability to produce victory in every spiritual battle, and I now have the power to overcome my flesh and the devil with Christ's authority vested in me. Unfortunately, many born again Christians do not walk in the victory that they have inherited through their faith in Jesus Christ. The assessment on their true spiritual condition cannot be determined by any man made formula. God is the only one who is qualified to judge the spiritual condition of an individual. Unlike man's judgment, the aggregate knowledge of God's judgment is always correct, fair, and merciful.

The "old man" of someone who is born again desires to have control. The soul (consisting of the mind, will, and emotions) of the new believer has to be put into submission to his spirit. Believers are justified when they look to Christ in faith. This faith produces genuine repentance of sin, and Christ's blood is applied to their eternal security. Since the soul consists of the three parts previously mentioned (all of which can be quite willful), it has to be brought into obedience. This process is referred to as sanctification. Justification is what Jesus Christ does for the believer, whereas sanctification is what He does in the believer after salvation. When someone is feeling guilty of sinful behavior they have already repented over, that is an indication of condemnation. Condemnation comes from the devil and he is referred to as the "Accuser of the Brethren." (Revelation 12:10) Conviction is what the inner man feels when his conscience declares him guilty of what he has done; or is contemplating on doing. The Holy Spirit within the new believer also chastises the born again man so that he will turn from unloving and sinful behavior. Any individual who professes to be a child of God and does not receive correction from Him is not born again. However, a believer can ignore these chastisements, if he so chooses.

When someone rejects the good news of salvation by faith in Jesus Christ the scriptures show us that a process of degeneration occurs within that individual's conscience. The end result is that the person believes the lie that there is nothing wrong with his sinful ways and that he is not accountable to God for his actions. (Romans 1:28)

If someone is capable of engaging in sinful activity without being convicted; he or she is in an extremely dangerous predicament. If the individual is a professing believer in Jesus Christ and continues to live in a way that is at odds with His character attributes, he is either immature in his faith, or he has not been born again. The good news is that if the Holy Spirit convicts him of sin then he has not been turned over to a reprobated mind. This type of mind is one that allows man to engage in perversion while believing that it is condoned by God. The Holy Spirit will not convict someone who has consciously made a decision to reject Him. It is necessary to note that many Christians are aware that they are living in a manner that is not God's best for them. However, it doesn't make them any less saved. Regardless of my opinion, if they are saved and continue to live in sin they will most likely be miserable.

The doctrine of the "spirit man" is taught all through the New Testament. It tells us that the new man (the "spirit man") is dead to sin, and can no longer continue in sin. This new man is not the outer man, but the inner man: I call him the spirit man. The spirit man wants to please his spiritual father, but the "old man" wants to fulfill its sinful desires. This is why Paul wrote the following to the church in Rome:

> "O wretched man that I am! Who will deliver me from this body of death? I thank God — through Jesus Christ our Lord!"
>
> Romans 7:24-25

In a following chapter Paul clearly stated that what Christ did allowed him to control his flesh through the renewing of his mind. The result of this renewing of the mind to what the word of God says contributed to his contentedness in every circumstance, and in making him capable of doing God's will.

> "I beseech you therefore, brethren, by the mercies of God, that you present your bodies a living sacrifice, holy, acceptable to God, which is your reasonable service. And do not be conformed to this world, but be transformed by the renewing of your mind, that you may prove what is that good and acceptable and perfect will of God."
>
> Roman 12:1-2

Paul habitually reiterated the importance of being renewed by the renovation and transformation of the mind. Meditating on God's word is one of the secrets to victorious Christian living. Therefore, the born again believer has no excuse to live a life dictated by the desires of the flesh.

There are Christian denominations that have adopted doctrines condoning the practice of perverted and progressively depraved sins. They are presently throwing off all restraints and are not being led by the Spirit, but by the flesh. How can organizations that claim to represent Christianity condone, encourage, and reward lifestyles that are clear abominations as shown in the word of God? I am concerned that many of their leaders may have never actually been born again! They have associated themselves with Jesus Christ, but the convicting presence of the Holy Spirit that is deposited in every saved man is not manifest in their decision making. These professing believers do not exhibit characteristic of being true Shepherds of the sheep; it seems they are concerned with their own personal agenda. They deceive their parishioners with doctrines that state that the grace of God is a license to throw off moral restraints and indulge in perversions. The judgment of these professed Christian leaders is reserved for God only. It is important to ensure all people are welcome in the body of Christ for fellowship regardless of sinful bondages, but without compromising the message of becoming a vessel of honor.

Refusal to Become a Vessel of Honor

Refusal to engage in the process of becoming a vessel of honor is an indication that the seed of Christ may not have been implanted in a person. There are passages in the Bible that prove that a life of purity is the expected result of becoming a believer. However, all have sinned and come short of the glory of God. Being in right-standing with God only comes by faith in the reconciliatory work of Jesus Christ. As Christians we all struggle with the infirmity of the flesh. The desire for the born again spirit to control the flesh is one manner God chastises His children. Someone who is born again cannot live in habitual sin without conviction. The First Epistle of John elaborates on this spiritual law and explains that God's love is manifested through the love of His given seed.

> Behold what manner of love the Father has bestowed on us, that we should be called children of God! Therefore the world does not know us, because it did not know Him. Beloved, now we are children of God; and it has not yet been revealed what we shall be, but we know that when He is revealed, we shall be like Him, for we shall see Him as He is. And everyone who has this hope in Him purifies himself, just as He is pure. Whoever commits sin also commits lawlessness, and sin is lawlessness. And you know that He was manifested to take away our sins, and in Him there is no sin. Whoever abides in Him does not sin. Whoever sins has neither seen Him nor known

Him. Little children, let no one deceive you. He who practices righteousness is righteous, just as He is righteous. He who sins is of the devil, for the devil has sinned from the beginning. For this purpose the Son of God was manifested, that He might destroy the works of the devil. Whoever has been born of God does not sin, for His seed remains in him; and he cannot sin, because he has been born of God.

1 John 3:1-9

I believe that "Sin" in the above passage of scripture refers to habitual acts of depravity without conviction, and trusting in acts of self righteousness to be in right-standing with God.

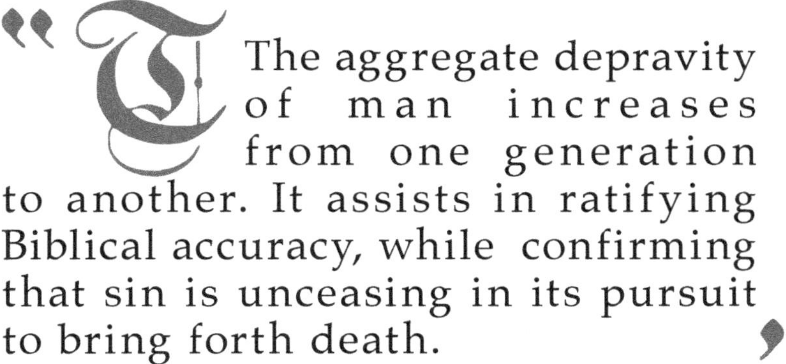

"The aggregate depravity of man increases from one generation to another. It assists in ratifying Biblical accuracy, while confirming that sin is unceasing in its pursuit to bring forth death."

When someone is genuinely born of God he is given benefits derived from righteousness. Some of these benefits are as follows:

- He has been given sonship by God the Father.
- He has been given freedom from sin and sickness.
- He has been given the ability to love the brethren.
- He has been given a true love for the ordinances of God.
- He has been given the power to fulfill God's law of love.
- He has been given the ability to overcome the curse of fallen man.
- He has been given the seed of Christ, and has been placed "In Him."
- He has been given the power to produce good fruit.

here are some professed believers in Jesus Christ within the universal body of Christ who have associated themselves with the Name of Christ, but who have never been placed "In Christ." These professed believers claim to know Jesus Christ and His will; however, they are actually wolves seeking the glory of men. I personally believe that many have been deceived by Satan, and really believe they are in right standing with God. These professed believers will have had ample opportunities to have become born again and be forgiven of their deceitfulness. They produce fruits that are the opposite of the fruits produced by the Holy Spirit, and seek to devour and scatter the sheep. They have never been genuinely born again and continue in works of unrighteousness without Godly conviction. These professed believers may be qualified to be recipients of the dreadful words that will be spoken by Jesus Christ at the great white throne judgment...

"I never knew you; depart from Me..."

Chapter Two

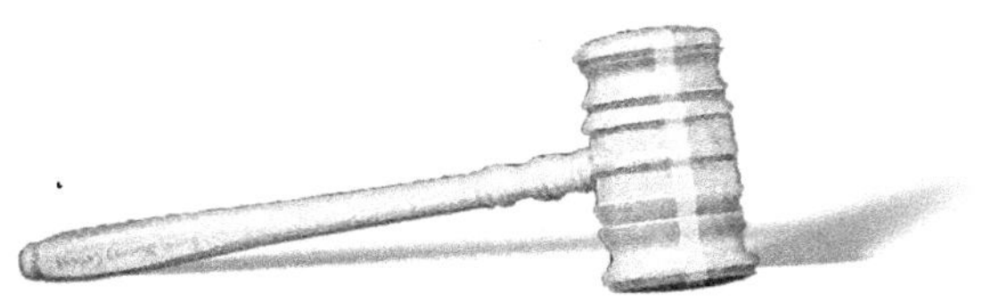

"...But He Who Does The WILL
Of My Father In Heaven..."
Matthew 7:21

In the early years of my Christianity I visited a church that one of my friends was a member of. This particular church contained great amounts of denominational legalism, and prided itself on upholding an uncompromising legalistic doctrine. I can remember my friend refusing to own a television set so that he could qualify to serve in the church based upon denominational standards. My friend was instructed that if he wanted to be in ministry he would be prohibited from owning a television or going to the movies. Dating anyone outside of his denomination was highly discouraged, and supporting radio and television ministries was unthinkable. This denomination removed itself from other Christian ministries, and those called to preach the Gospel in that church were limited to serving only within that denomination.

In contrast, the personal convictions of the Apostle Paul were not forced on the Saints, and he strived to remove bondages from them. Many religious denominations add requirements that put their parishioners in bondage. These religious rules are open doors for the spirit of self-righteousness to deceive their parishioners. I am not advocating a spirit of rebellion towards church leadership through refusing to submit to their authority; however, people are precious and should not be controlled by tyrants. (1 Peter 5:1-5) Many such tyrants will proclaim that God has given them a "personal revelation" that those who depart from their spiritual covering will be devoured by Satan. These tyrants preach that when a person leaves their protection that he is in direct rebellion to the will of God. (Some may be stepping out of the place God has planned for them to be, however, many will be called to serve in other ministry offices.) It is not uncommon for denominations in which tyrants thrive to instruct their parishioners on how to live their personal lives. These tyrants will instruct their followers on who they can marry, what they can purchase, and even how often they can have sexual relations with their spouses. Many of these tyrants will have some scriptures that they use to justify their belief that they are to control the lives of their parishioners. The Apostle Peter digresses on the characteristics that all ministerial leaders must possess, and records them in his Epistle 1 Peter 5:1-5.

> I WARN and counsel the elders among you (the pastors and spiritual guides of the church) as a fellow elder and as an eyewitness [called to testify] of the sufferings of Christ, as well as a sharer in the glory (the honor and splendor) that is to

> be revealed (disclosed, unfolded): Tend (nurture, guard, guide, and fold) the flock of God that is [your responsibility], not by coercion or constraint, but willingly; not dishonorably motivated by the advantages and profits [belonging to the office], but eagerly and cheerfully; Not domineering [as arrogant, dictatorial, and overbearing persons] over those in your charge, but being examples (patterns and models of Christian living) to the flock (the congregation). And [then] when the Chief Shepherd is revealed, you will win the conqueror's crown of glory." (The Amplified Bible)
>
> 1 Peter 5:1-5

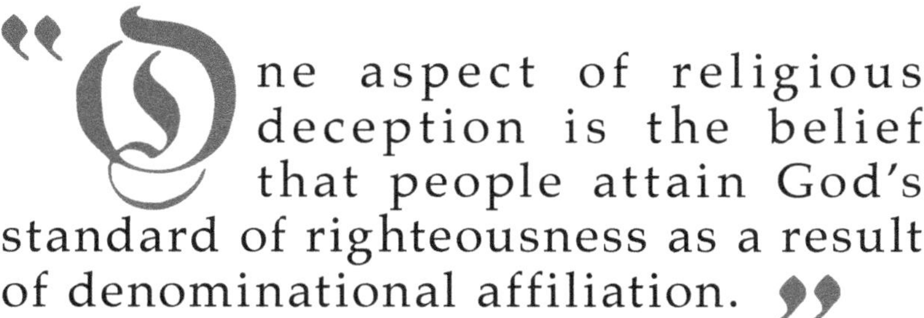

"One aspect of religious deception is the belief that people attain God's standard of righteousness as a result of denominational affiliation."

The Prophet Jeremiah recorded a passage of scripture that serves as a warning to pastors who treat their parishioners harshly and fail to care for them properly.

> [1]"Woe to the shepherds who are destroying and
> scattering the sheep of my pasture!" declares
> the Lord. [2]Therefore this is what the Lord, the
> God of Israel, says to the shepherds who tend
> my people: "Because you have scattered my flock

> and driven them away and have not bestowed care on them, I will bestow punishment on you for the evil you have done," declares the Lord. [3]"I myself will gather the remnant of my flock out of all the countries where I have driven them and will bring them back to their pasture, where they will be fruitful and increase in number. [4]I will place shepherds over them who will tend them, and they will no longer be afraid or terrified, nor will any be missing," declares the Lord.
>
> Jeremiah 23:1-4 (NIV)

I encourage Christians to study the scriptures in the same manner the Berean Christians did as recorded in *Acts 17:11, "[The Bereans] were more noble than those in Thessalonica, in that they received the word with all readiness of mind, and searched the scriptures daily, whether those things were so." (KJV)* It is better to leave a denomination that is controlled by tyrants than to stay a member and cause divisions. Through study and admonishment from the word of God and fellow Christians, respectively, I have learned that the will of God is not fulfilled through the adherence of man-made religious rules.

The Will of God

The will of God has been established by the New Covenant through the payment of the blood of Jesus Christ. The Bible has recorded many covenants that God has made with mankind, including the following:

1. The covenant with Adam, recorded in Genesis 2.
2. The covenant with Noah, recorded in Genesis 9.
3. The covenant with Abraham, recorded in Genesis 15.
4. The covenant with Moses, recorded in Exodus 19.
5. The covenant relating to the promised land, recorded in Deuteronomy 30.
6. The covenant with David, recorded in 2nd Samuel 7.
7. The New Covenant, recorded in Jeremiah 31. (Covenant made with all those who are born again.)

All of God's Biblical covenants contain promises to the beneficiaries. Those promises are the will of God for the recipients of the covenant. It is obligatory for the beneficiaries of the covenant to know what it says. The word "covenant" comes from the Greek word *Diatheke,* which translated literally means a contract or testament. It is specifically used when referring to the last will and testament of someone who has died. Within the covenant all parties are held to the agreement made to one another. The functionality of the agreement depends upon all parties fulfilling their respective parts of the agreement.

God made a covenant with Abraham as recorded in Genesis 15. The covenant included benefits for Abraham's health, prosperity, and recognition before God as being righteous.

The covenant God made with Abraham was inaugurated with the blood of sacrificial animals. However; sin could not permanently be atoned for by the blood of animals. That is why Jesus Christ walked through the spread out carcasses of these sacrificed animals, making an agreement with God and Himself. *(Genesis 15:9-21)* This act constituted Christ's acceptance of the plan that would qualify all Nations for the opportunity to be forgiven of their sins.

> For the life of the flesh is in the blood, and I have given it to you upon the altar to make atonement for your souls; for it is the blood that makes atonement for the soul.
>
> Leviticus 17:11

Jesus agreed to pay the obligatory payment that simultaneously fulfilled the Old Covenant, and put into force the New Covenant.

> Likewise He also took the cup after supper, saying, 'This cup is the new covenant in My blood, which is shed for you.'
>
> Luke 22:20-21

The payment rendered was Christ's blood. *(Hebrews 10)* The beneficiaries of the contract are those who are counted righteous through faith in Jesus Christ. The Old Covenant God had with Abraham was merely a foreshadowing of the better Covenant to come, which allowed the Jews to be justified by faith in the coming Messiah. When Jesus fulfilled His promise as Messiah, all of humanity was eligible to be justified through faith in Him. Jesus walked through the spread out pieces of the sacrificial animals as a foreshadowing of the payment that had sealed an agreement with Him and God. *(See Genesis 15:17-21)* The unimaginable plan of redemption that was concealed in the Old Testament became revealed after Christ's resurrection from the dead. In essence: God made an agreement with Himself, and is the living executor of His own Will. God did all of this on the behalf of mankind and provided a process by which to redeem humanity without compromising His Holiness. Therefore, the essence of properly knowing how to do the will of God is disclosed in His effective, binding, and authoritative covenant. *(See: Hebrews 9:16-22, Galatians 3:16-19)*

Freedom from the consequences of guilt and condemnation is established in both the Old Covenant and New Covenants in much the same manner. Abraham was justified in the Old Covenant by faith in God. *(Roman 4:3)* The eternal benefits of the covenant depended on the fulfillment of a pre-destined Messiah (Jesus Christ). The payment for the sin of mankind still had to be rendered in both. In addition, the death of the Messiah allowed the benefits of the will to be applied to the recipients. The recipients of the Old and New Covenants are those who have been justified by faith.

> That the blessing of Abraham might come upon the Gentiles in Christ Jesus, that we might receive the promise of the Spirit through faith.
>
> Galatians 3:14

The beneficiaries of the will are required to reach an age of maturity before they are permitted access to certain benefits willed to them. If they have not reached an age of accountability they will be required to wait before they can draw on their inheritance. When there is a benefit available to the beneficiary that they are unaware exists, the executor of the will provides them with awareness. The executor of Christ's Will is Himself, and He has provided all notifications (and awareness) of His Will through His word and Spirit. Therefore, beneficiaries that do not know God's word and the Holy Spirit are withheld access to their inheritance because of their lack of knowledge. The Apostle Paul understood that an heir to a throne is prohibited from accessing his inheritance until he is proven mature.

> Now I say that the heir, as long as he is a child, does not differ at all from a slave, though he is master of all, but is under guardians and stewards until the time appointed by the father.
>
> Galatians 4:1-2

The Mosaic Covenant

The covenant God made with Moses was an addition to the agreement made with Abraham. The Ten Commandments given to Moses were used as a guideline for righteousness for the Israelites. *(Galatians 3:24-25)* They exposed the Israelites' incapability to meet the standard of righteousness that God requires, and insured that the Israelites would realize their need for a Savior. The Ten Commandments are still used to expose the inadequacy of men who have not accepted Jesus Christ as their redeemer before God. The Holy Spirit then draws them to the cross after they have realized their incapability to redeem themselves. Immediately after repentance of their sins and acceptance of Christ through faith occurs; they are freed from the curse of the law.

> Christ has redeemed us from the curse of the law, having become a curse for us (for it is written, 'Cursed is everyone who hangs on a tree').
>
> Galatians 3:13

God's Will Fulfilled

Jesus did not desire to go to the cross, and had the opportunity not to do the will of the Father in the Garden of Gethsemane. But God's plan of redemption continued when Jesus prayed; *"Not my will, but your will be done." (Mark 14:36)* Preceding the betrayal and arrest of Jesus in the Garden of Gethsemane; Jesus prayed with such weightiness that it is recorded that his sweat became like great drops of blood. *(Luke 22:44)* Jesus did not desire to be murdered mercilessly, but He did desire to do the will of His Father. The redeemer of mankind chose to be crucified because he loves His Father and mankind with more esteem then He loves Himself. If Christians love God more then they love themselves; they will be willing to pray: "Not my will, but your will be done." A genuine desire to please God is one prerequisite for God releasing His fullest blessings in the life of a Christian.

Jesus repeatedly stated in His teachings that He was doing the will of His Father who had sent Him. In the Gospel of John 5:30, Jesus told those who followed the law of Moses that His actions were the will of His Father.

> "I can of Myself do nothing. As I hear, I judge; and My judgment is righteous, because I do not seek My own will but the will of the Father who sent Me."
>
> John 5:30

The parables spoken by Jesus to the multitudes were explained in great detail to his chosen beloved. *(Mark 4:33)* The disciples were being prepared to establish God's will throughout the earth which would commence after Jesus Christ resurrected from the dead and the Holy Spirit was sent. The ways that the will of God is revealed include, but are not limited to, the following:

1. The acts and commands of Jesus Christ.

2. The teachings of Jesus Christ reiterated by the Apostles.

3. The will of God manifested by the Holy Spirit and His written word.

4. Discerning God's desire through prayer.

Judged as Being a Hypocrite

One day I was judged by a professing believer in Jesus Christ as being a hypocrite. He felt compelled to tell me that I was not a true Christian, and expanded this statement by declaring that a true Christian would have a joyous countenance radiating from his face. At the time, I had been meditating on a book that I had recently read regarding Hell. I was sorrowful in my spirit as I looked around at my fellow co-workers and realized that many of them exhibited no evidence of knowing God. As a result, the expression on my face was not a joyful one. I lovingly asked him, "Do you think Jesus Christ had a joyous countenance on His face when he was being crucified on the Cross of Calvary, while Roman soldiers were piercing iron spikes through His body? I then asked him when the last time was that he went out witnessing in his neighborhood telling people about the promises available to them in God's word. I inquired if he had ever given a sacrificial love offering to a brother in need, made a commitment to lay his life down as a living sacrifice for the purposes of God in His life, and if he had ever prayed for the sick by laying his hands on them so that they would be healed. I then reminded him that a true disciple of Jesus Christ is not judged by the countenance on one's face, but by how faithful one is in doing the will of God as revealed through the acts of Jesus Christ. Christians are to be joyous and thankful for what they have been given in Christ, but to judge someone's commitment to Jesus Christ and His obedience to the will of God based on his facial expression is sinful. Jesus told a crowd of people surrounding Him that those who do the will of His Father are the true members of His family. (Mark 3:31-34) Jesus told his disciples that they would not only do the same things he was doing, but even greater things. This was a prophetic word given to the apostles, and extended to all those who would believe in Him. *John 14:12-14 "Most assuredly, I say to you, he who believes in Me, the works that I do he will do also; and greater works than these he will do, because I go to My Father. And whatever you ask in My name, that I will do, that the Father may be glorified in the Son. If you ask anything in My name, I will do it."*

The actions of Jesus Christ as recorded in the canonized gospels are the outward manifestations of God's will. The desire to do God's will is accessed by becoming matured in Jesus Christ. This accessibility is accomplished through growing into a living example of Jesus Christ and becoming a personification of the will of God. Manifestations of God's will are shown to the world by Christians doing what Jesus did. Those who proclaim a gospel message that does not reflect the will of God as manifested through His Last Will and Testament may be wolves in sheep's clothing.

Jesus Manifested the Will of God Through Healing

God's will is that all people would live a life free from sickness and disease. Sickness and disease are byproducts of the curse of Adam. The word sickness in the Greek is *Astheneo*; it conveys the meaning of being weak and feeble. Implicit in the definition of the word is mental anguish and worriedness. The Greek word for disease is *Astheneia*, and it conveys the idea of someone not whole within himself. Those who were sick with leprosy as recorded in the New Testament were diseased (*Astheneia*). When someone doesn't know that God's will is for them to be healthy, they are susceptible to sickness. The significance of what Jesus Christ accomplished for the right to divine health for those who believe in Him can be found in the word "Saved." The word save in the Greek is *Sozo*. In the Bible it is used interchangeably with the Greek word for "salvation." This interchangeably represents redemption of man *and* freedom from sickness and disease through healing. The benefits include complete empowerment for success and the promise of divine health. If one confesses with his mouth the Lord Jesus, and believes in his heart that God raised Christ from the dead, he will be **healed** (*Sozo*). *(Romans 10:9)* Jesus always manifested the will of God to all those who came to Him in faith. In Matthew 8:1-4, Jesus healed a man with leprosy who stated his belief that Jesus could heal him if He wanted to. Jesus responded by telling the man that His will was to heal him. It is interesting to note that after Jesus healed the diseased man, Jesus told him to testify to the priest that he had been made whole. If Jesus were walking the earth today, I believe He would have sent the man to church leaders who believe it is not the will of God for all to be healed.

> [1]When He had come down from the mountain, great multitudes followed Him. [2]And behold, a leper came and worshiped Him, saying, "Lord, if You are willing, You can make me clean." [3]Then Jesus put out His hand and touched him, saying, "I am willing; be cleansed." Immediately his leprosy was cleansed. [4]And Jesus said to him, "See that you tell no one; but go your way, show yourself to the priest, and offer the gift that Moses commanded, as a testimony to them."
>
> Matthew: 8 1-4

Denying that the will of God is to heal people, as revealed through the canonized scriptures, is heresy. Healing is a covenant benefit and is included in the reconciliatory work of Jesus Christ. The book of Numbers 21:7-9 records an event that occurred to the Hebrew people in which they had spoken against the Lord, and as a result poisonous serpents entered into their camp. (It's interesting to note that the serpents had always been outside the camp, but that it was not until the Israelites lost trust in God that the serpents entered.) The people then came to Moses in repentance, resulting in Moses making a petition to God for their deliverance. God responded to Moses by instructing him to make a brass image of a serpent and to fasten it upon a pole. He told him to instruct the Israelites to look upon the image if they were bitten, and to tell them that if they did, they would live. Moses was obedient to the will of God, and did as he was instructed to do. Every person that looked upon the serpent of brass was healed. I believe more Christians would be healed if they would repent, trust, and receive the spoken word of God in faith. (Divine Health is obtained by faith; *Mark 5:34, 11:22-24*) However, only God knows why someone does not ultimately receive divine healing. We have to be truthful and say that even though it is clearly God's will to heal, we just don't know everything He knows.

The Gospel of John 3:14-17 shows a correlation between what occurred in regards to healing for the Hebrew people and the healing available to all those who look to the Cross for their complete deliverance.

> 14And as Moses lifted up the serpent in the wilder-
> ness, even so must the Son of Man be lifted up,
> 15that whoever believes in Him should not perish
> but have eternal life. 16For God so loved the world
> that He gave His only begotten Son, that who-
> ever believes in Him should not perish but have
> everlasting life. 17For God did not send His Son
> into the world to condemn the world, but that the

> world through Him might be ***saved*** [also healed; Gk. Soza] *(Emphasis Mine)*
>
> John 3:14-17

The prophet Isaiah was cognizant of the fact that the future Messiah would be wounded and stricken for the purposes of doing God's will. One way Jesus Christ accomplished God's will was through restoring mankind to complete (*Soza*) wholeness. Jesus Christ was prophesied hundreds of years before He stepped out of Heaven into the body God prepared for Him—and so was the fact that He brought healing.

> Therefore, when He came into the world, He said; Sacrifice and offering You did not desire, but a body You have prepared for Me. In burnt offerings and sacrifices for sin You had no pleasure. Then I said, 'Behold, I have come — In the volume of the book it is written of Me — To do Your will, O God.'
>
> Hebrews 10:5-7

The will of God to heal humanity was concealed in His Old Testament prophesies. Isaiah Chapter 53: 4-5 shows us that the predicted Messiah would provide deliverance from sickness and disease.

> Surely He has borne our griefs and carried our sorrows; Yet we esteemed Him stricken, Smitten by God, and afflicted. 5 But He was wounded for

> our transgressions, He was bruised for our iniquities; The chastisement for our peace was upon Him, And by His stripes we are healed. (NKJV)
>
> Isaiah 53:4-5

There is vigorous debate in Christendom over whether or not it is the will of God to have humanity healed from their sicknesses and diseases. Many Christian denominations are adamant on standing by their doctrine that healing ceased with the first Christian Church, and was used solely for the catapulting of the great commission given by Jesus Christ. The logical response to this false doctrine would be to inquire if the great commission's objectives have been accomplished. If the great commission had been fulfilled, then the dispensation of the Church would have ended. The dispensation of the Church is still valid. The command to evangelize the entire world and make disciples of all nations, baptizing them in the name of the Father, the Son, and the Holy Spirit has not been rescinded, so neither has divine healing. *(Matthew 28:18-20)*

The Apostle Peter was well aware that the blood of Jesus has within it the properties of healing atonement, and referenced Isaiah 53:4-5 and expanded by stating that Jesus Christ is the fulfillment of Isaiah's prophesy. The following passage of scripture was written to Jews who had converted to Christianity.

> 21 For to this you were called, because Christ also
> suffered for us, leaving us an example, that you
> should follow His steps: 22 "Who committed no sin,
> Nor was deceit found in His mouth"; 23 who, when
> He was reviled, did not revile in return; when He
> suffered, He did not threaten, but committed
> Himself to Him who judges righteously; 24 who
> Himself bore our sins in His own body on the tree,
> that we, having died to sins, might live for righ-
> teousness — by whose stripes you were healed.
> 25 For you were like sheep going astray, but have
> now returned to the Shepherd and Overseer of
> your souls.
>
> 1 Peter 2:21-25

Many theologians will quote scriptures that are related to the suffering of the Saints. It is essential to comprehend that those scriptures are not referring to physical sickness. As I pointed out in chapter one, many of the first century Saints were being persecuted. The afflictions and sufferings they encountered were the persecutions they endured for their faith in Jesus Christ.

If it is not the will of God for all people to be healthy then the logical conclusion is that every practicing physician, scientist, and professional working in the medical field is in opposition to the will of God. Some Christian leaders preach the false doctrine that God is glorified in their sickness. My question to them is: why would anyone want to serve a God who makes him sick? If it is the will of God for people to be sick, why didn't Jesus go around laying hands on people speaking sickness and disease into their lives? It would have been the logical thing to do if it was the will of His Father. Jesus did not go to those who were healthy and say, "Receive leprosy, your faith has made you sick." Professed Christian leaders who discourage divine healing are in rebellion to the will of God, and are engaged in activities that are the direct antithesis of God's will. The lack of healing manifestations is not an indication of God's will for them to be sick. *Matthew 12:15 "But when Jesus knew it, He withdrew from there. And great multitudes followed Him, and He healed them all."* An assiduous academic study of the New and Old Testaments will reveal that Jesus Christ is the healer of those who come to Him in faith.

What Jesus Christ Did

The following is a list of some things that Jesus Christ did being obedient to the will of God:

1. Trained His disciples to do the will of God. (Luke 5:1-11)

2. Ministered to the multitudes. (Luke 6:17)

3. Calmed a Storm. (Luke 8: 22-25)

4. Cast out demons from those who were afflicted. (Luke 8:26-33)

5. Sent out Apostles. (Luke 9:1-6)
6. Fed the hungry. (Luke 9:10-21)
7. Taught that if one is to be great, he must become the least. (Luke 9:46-48)
8. Advised cities to repent from their sin or perish. (Luke 10:13-16)
9. Rejoiced in the Holy Spirit. (Luke 10:21-22)
10. Taught His disciples to pray. (Luke 11:1-13)
11. Rebuked religious people who made the word of God of no effect. (Luke 11)
12. Warned His disciples of hypocritical religious people. (Luke 12)
13. Taught people the secret of how not to worry. (Luke 12:22-34)
14. Told all to repent, and that if they didn't, they would perish in their sins. (Luke 13:1-5)
15. Upset the religious leaders by putting people before ritual. (Luke 14:1-6)
16. Advised large crowds to count the cost of following Him. (Luke 14:25-33)
17. Warned the multitudes of hell. (Luke:19-31)

18. Told His servants of their duty to do His will. (Luke 17:7-10)

19. Warned against the coveting of money. (Luke 18:18-25)

20. Prohibited His house (the Temple) from being used for the purposes of commerce. (Luke 19)

21. Warned of being overly concerned with everyday life. (Luke 21:34-36)

22. Was crucified and forgave His murderers. (Luke 23:26-44)

23. Proclaimed that He was the Messiah. (Luke 24:44-49)

24. Commanded people to tithe. (Matthew 23:23 & Luke 11:42)

25. Proclaimed that all must be born again to enter heaven. (John 3:3)

26. Forgave adulterous women. (John 1-11)

27. Proclaimed that He was God. (John 8)

28. Raised the dead. (John 11)

29. Wept and grieved with his family. (John 11:28)

30. Made decisions based on purpose and not feelings. (John 12:27-32)

31. Gave a new commandment: to love one another, like He loves. (John 13:31)

32. Proclaimed the works of the Holy Spirit. (John 16:4-14)

33. Rebuked Peter for comparing himself to others. (John 2:21-24)

34. Was baptized in water. (Matthew 3:13-15)

35. Told His disciples that the Holy Spirit will give them power. (Acts 1:6-8)

36. Disapproved of the practice of divorce by convenience. (Mark 19:8)

37. Overcame temptation. (Mark 4:1)

38. Fasted. (Mark 4:18)

39. Wept for the crimes Israel committed against him. (Luke 19:41-44)

40. Gave the Greatest commandment: love God completely. (Matthew 22:34)

> "But why do you call Me 'Lord, Lord,' and not do the things which I say?"
>
> Luke 6:46

The expression of God's will is revealed through Jesus Christ. The way He loved the multitudes, healed the sick, grieved with the afflicted, and instructed humanity to live is a pattern for all people to follow.

Early Days of Discipleship

When I first came to know Jesus Christ I assisted a beloved brother in the Lord with delivering newspapers. We would pick up the newspapers at around 3:00 a.m. every morning and proceed with counting, folding, and delivering them. While in the car during those early morning hours he would impart to me all he had learned about the Bible, and about flowing in the will of God. He was very committed in his faith, and had been serving Jesus Christ for approximately five years. His testimony was encouraging, and he would pray for people's healing habitually. I vividly remember a time when he prayed for a man's leg and it was healed. This brother in Jesus Christ played an active role in ensuring that I received the "Baptism in the Holy Spirit," with evidence of speaking in unknown tongues. He instructed me on how to engage in spiritual warfare when my faith was being proven. I had an opportunity to see faithfulness in action through him. Self-sacrifice was shown to me every morning when he got up to deliver those newspapers. He refused to take well-paying, prestigious jobs that would interfere with the Church service times. Therefore, he did what was available to him, and paid his rent with the wages from the paper-route. It did not stop there, but between his regular job, being faithful to all services, raising a family, serving in church ministry, and doing the paper-route, he lived on about 4 hours of sleep a day.

Discipleship of new believers in Jesus Christ is essential to fulfilling the will of God. Jesus Christ spent copious amounts of time teaching His twelve disciples. Their success after He rose from the dead was the result of His discipleship of them. The disciples were actively involved in conducting the will of God by leading people to Him. They evangelized with fervency, and were successful fishers of men. Furthermore, they understood that the will of God is that no one would go to Hell, and that all would come to repentance. Jesus showed His disciples the will of God by manifesting it through His actions.

The definition of "disciple" is a disciplined student, beginner, or apprentice. A disciple is someone who is being instructed with the objective of becoming like his teacher. Jesus Christ is the teacher of all disciples, and He uses more mature believers in Him to assist in the discipleship process. The book of Acts is often referred to with its unabridged title, 'The Acts of the Apostles.' One can assume that the Apostles were actively engaged in carrying out the will of God by *doing* something. They had hands on training with Jesus Christ, witnessed His ministry, death, resurrection, and ascension into Heaven. Who would be better qualified to express the will of Jesus Christ?

The Precious Holy Spirit

The will of God is manifested through the acts of the Holy Spirit. The Holy Spirit is the third person of the Trinity. He is a sensitive individual that always assists in the will of the Father. He leads born again saints into the ministries that God has called them to. He is the still small voice that guides believers away from danger. He is the constraining force that keeps God's children on the right path. The Holy Spirit is the administrator of all the spiritual gifts given to the saints for the edification of the Church. The Holy Spirit was promised to the believers by Jesus Christ before He ascended up to Heaven. He is the person of the Trinity who draws people to repentance and faith in Jesus Christ. The Holy Spirit convicts mankind of sin through their conscience and reveals salvation through the redemptive plan of Jesus Christ.

While driving down Interstate 10 in Tucson AZ, I was consumed by an overwhelming thought that I needed to exit at the upcoming ramp. I attempted to discard this leading to exit because I had an appointment to fulfill. As I was getting closer to the exit ramp the leading got stronger; at the last opportunity I exited the interstate. After I came to the stop sign the still small voice within me said, "Turn right, then go straight, when you get to the second street make a right turn. Drive down that neighborhood until you find a park. I have set up a divine appointment for you to introduce someone to Jesus Christ." I followed the instructions of the still small voice that were revealed through my conscience, and discovered a small park in a poorer neighborhood of the city. (1 Peter 3:21) I noticed a man approximately 30 years old who was sitting on a park bench. The man was eating his lunch, and it appeared to me that he was a landscape employee. I called him over to me, and quickly realized that he was only capable of conversing in Spanish. I had recently put some gospel materials which were written in Spanish in my ministerial witnessing bag. I conversed with the man in Spanish for about 5 minutes, and told him how to receive Jesus Christ. The man was open to the message of salvation, and relayed to me his desire to have a personal relationship with God. After the man was properly introduced to Jesus Christ, I gave him a Spanish Bible and literature explaining how to commence his new life in Jesus Christ. The Spirit of God dwells within every born again believer leading and assisting them in discerning the will of the Father. *Proverbs 20:27 states; "The spirit of a man is the lamp of the Lord, Searching all the inner depths of his heart."*

The Holy Spirit ministers through people who are obedient to His leading. Flowing in the will of God is attainable by understanding that the Holy Spirit is dwelling within the believer. The Apostle Paul instructed the Church in Corinth that the Spirit of God was given to the true believers in Jesus Christ for the purpose of partaking in the innermost sentiments of God. *(1 Corinthians 2:9-16)* The Holy Spirit must be abiding in an individual for the individual to be saved. *(Roman 8:9)* Many people are determining their eternal security based on membership status in an acknowledged Christian church. There is no recorded instruction in the Bible that states; "If you are a recognized member of a Christian Church, you will be saved."

What the Early Saints Did

A study of the Apostles' actions will also reveal the will of God. The Holy Spirit was deposited within them as they ventured out to introduce the world to Jesus Christ. Liberality was given to the Holy Spirit for Him to manifest the will of God through signs and wonders. The Apostles and their disciples were used as vessels by the Holy Spirit.

The Apostles and Disciples manifested the will of God in the following ways:

1. Preached the Crucifixion of Jesus Christ. (Act:2:23)
2. Spoke with new tongues (Acts 2:4)
3. Laid hands on the sick. (Acts 3:9)
4. Proclaimed the Deity of Jesus Christ. (Acts 3:12)
5. Were persecuted for their faith in Jesus Christ. (Acts 4)
6. Were imprisoned for their faith in Jesus Christ. (Acts 5)
7. Experienced great growth of the Church. (Acts 6:7)

8. Rebuked hypocritical religious people. (Acts 7:1-56)
9. Preached the New Covenant of God. (Acts 7:1-56)
10. Forgave their murderers while they were being stoned. (Act 7:87-60)
11. Baptized new disciples. (Acts 8:13), (Acts 8:36)
12. Heard the voice of God in regards to missions. (Acts 9:4)
13. Ministered the baptism of the Holy Spirit to new believers. (Acts 9:17)
14. Prayed for the deliverance of imprisoned saints. (Acts 12:5)
15. Saw Jesus as the fulfillment of Old Testament Messianic prophecy. (Acts 13)
16. Started new churches. (Acts13:46)
17. Condemned idolatry. (Acts 17:28-30)
18. Partook of the Lord's supper (Acts 20:7-8)
19. Warned of wolves that would attempt to divide the Church. (Acts 20:28)
20. Were led by the Holy Spirit on where to go. (Acts 20)
21. Received visions from the Holy Spirit. (Acts 22:17)

22. Received Holy Spirit manifestations in the form of prophecy. (Acts 21)

23. Informed all future believers they were eligible to be filled with the Holy Spirit. (Acts 2:38-39)

24. Were used as vessels by the Holy Spirit to perform healing miracles. (Acts 3:8)

25. Received commandments from Jesus Christ on how to implement His will. (Acts 2:2)

The acts of the apostles were outward expressions of the will of God. The preceding list of actions carried out through them records only a smattering of all they did. It is obvious that the Holy Spirit assisted them in the same fashion that He assisted Jesus Christ in His ministry. The Holy Spirit desires to assist those of all Christian denominations in the same manner. Unbiased scholars of the Bible would concur that the will of God is manifested through the outpouring of the Holy Spirit. The Holy Spirit in His infinite wisdom and desire to draw all men to Jesus Christ uses the Saints of God for the purposes of the Father. I will note that not all the Holy Spirit did is recorded in the Bible. Some scholars maintain that the Holy Spirit only did the things listed in the Bible. That cannot be true because everyone who has ever come to Jesus was drawn by the Holy Spirit. The ability to record all the manifestations of the Holy Spirit that occurred with the first Christian Church was not feasible.

They did not have the option of recording events with the aid of computers and other technological advancements. I believe that the Holy Spirit conducted countless manifestations of the will of God during the period of the early Church. However, the manifestations were not recorded because of the difficulty of the task. The Holy Spirit desires to have fellowship with all believers all the time!

Many Professed Christians Grieve the Holy Spirit

Professing Christian denominations that are prohibiting the flow of the Holy Spirit in their services, programs, and missionary projects are wounding Him. He has been sent from above to assist the Church in the manifestation of the will of God. Unfortunately, many Christian religionists are more concerned with not offending someone in the Church than with inviting the Holy Spirit to manifest the will of the Father. As a result, they are grieving the Holy Spirit, and transgressing against the will of God.

The will of God is for you to be truthful even if it causes you to suffer. This principle became evident to me when I decided to be truthful after I was asked why I had not reported to work. I had worked a double shift the night before, and I was unable to rest properly the following morning. I was required to return to work in eight hours, and I just did not want to report. When I told my supervisor of my unwillingness to report that day, he asked me why. I told him that I just didn't feel like driving to work because I was exhausted. The supervisor informed me that my excuse was not valid, and I was informed that if I didn't report I would be marked as absent without approval, and that my pay would be docked. It was common practice for my fellow co-workers to call in sick after working double shifts. I had been working there for over a year and had not used any of my accrued sick-leave. After becoming frustrated because of the incident, I shared it with a brother in the Lord. He showed me through scripture that it is the will of God for a believer to tell the truth, even if he suffers. *(1 Peter 3:17)* If I would have called in sick, I would have been lying. My conscience would have convicted me, and I would have been guilty of transgressing against the word of God. I had chosen to tell the truth regardless of the consequences.

The will of the Father is expressed through the scriptures found in the Bible. The Bible instructs us on how to live honorably before God and man. It is divinely inspired by God and has immeasurable amounts of wisdom contained within it.

> All Scripture is given by inspiration of God, and is profitable for doctrine, for reproof, for correction, for instruction in righteousness, that the man of God may be complete, thoroughly equipped for every good work.
>
> 2 Timothy 3:16-17

When a Christian looks into the mirror of God's word he sees Jesus Christ. When he walks away from the word of God he is reminded not to forget that he looks just like Him. The essence of God's will and the Holy Spirit is deposited within the believer when he is born again, and that is who he is in Christ. The problem is that when the believer walks away from the mirror he forgets who he really is in Christ, and acts like his pre-saved natural man. Christians who do not spend quality time reading and studying the Bible are limited in their ability to discern the will of God. True religion is not manifested in them because they are not serving in love towards those that are unable to care for themselves. The cares of the world have taken their time and curtailed their ability to serve in a Christ-like manner.

> 22Do not merely listen to the word, and so deceive
> yourselves. Do what it says. 23Anyone who listens
> to the word but does not do what it says is like a
> man who looks at his face in a mirror 24and, after
> looking at himself, goes away and immediately
> forgets what he looks like. 25But the man who
> looks intently into the perfect law that gives freedom, and continues to do this, not forgetting what
> he has heard, but doing it — he will be blessed
> in what he does. 26If anyone considers himself
> religious and yet does not keep a tight rein on
> his tongue, he deceives himself and his religion is
> worthless. 27Religion that God our Father accepts

as pure and faultless is this: to look after orphans and widows in their distress and to keep oneself from being polluted by the world.

James 1:22-27 (NIV)

It is the Will of God to Make a Stand for Christ

But the Pharisees and lawyers rejected the will of God for themselves, not having been baptized by him.

Luke 7:30

It is the Will of God to go to Church

[10]Making request if, by some means, now at last I may find a way in the will of God to come to you. [11]For I long to see you, that I may impart to you some spiritual gift, so that you may be established — [12]that is, that I may be encouraged together with you by the mutual faith both of you and me.

Romans 1:10-12

[24]And let us consider one another in order to stir up love and good works, [25]not forsaking the assembling of ourselves together, as is the manner of some, but exhorting one another, and so much the more as you see the Day approaching.

Hebrews10:24-25

It is the will of God to Speak in Tongues

> [26]Likewise the Spirit also helps in our weaknesses. For we do not know what we should pray for as we ought, but the Spirit Himself makes intercession for us with groanings which cannot be uttered. [27]Now He who searches the hearts knows what the mind of the Spirit is, because He makes intercession for the saints according to the will of God.
>
> Romans 8:26-27

It is the will of God to Present Your Body a Living Sacrifice to God

> [1]I beseech you therefore, brethren, by the mercies of God, that you present your bodies a living sacrifice, holy, acceptable to God, which is your reasonable service. [2]And do not be conformed to this world, but be transformed by the renewing of your mind, that you may prove what is that good and acceptable and perfect will of God.
>
> Romans12:1-2

It is the Will of God to Abstain from Sexual Immorality

> [3]For this is the will of God, your sanctification: that you should abstain from sexual immorality; [4]that each of you should know how to possess his own vessel in sanctification and honor, [5]not

> in passion of lust, like the Gentiles who do not know God
>
> 1 Thessalonians 4:3-5

It is the Will of God to Rejoice, Pray, and Give Thanks in Abundance

> Rejoice always, 17 pray without ceasing, 18 in everything give thanks; for this is the will of God in Christ Jesus for you. 19 Do not quench the Spirit...
>
> 1 Thessalonians 5:16-19

It is the Will of God for all men to be saved

> 4 Who will have all men to be saved, and to come unto the knowledge of the truth. (KJV)
>
> 1 Timothy 2:4

My First Holy Confession

In the year 1979 at the age of eight years old I had my first "Holy Communion." One prerequisite to having my first communion was engaging in a practice known as confession. On the Saturday morning I was scheduled to complete the ritual, I had forgotten that I was required to be at the Church at 10:00 a.m. that morning. I was disheveled because I had been attempting to build a tree house with scraps from my father's workshop, and I generally looked like someone who had been rolling around in the dirt. I decided to take the shorter route to the church even though it required me to run up a steeper incline. I accidentally stepped into a mud puddle which contributed to my already disheveled appearance. By the time I arrived at the church, I was sweating profusely. The other children were lined up outside the confessional waiting for their opportunity to confess all of their sins to the Priest. The children were arrayed like their parents who were wearing their best Sunday morning church apparel. I took my place in the line feeling as if all the other children and parents were looking down upon me. Finally, my turn to enter the confessional arrived. I was concerned that I would appear sinful before the Priest because I was not arrayed like the other children. I then kneeled down and said the sentence that I had memorized, "Bless me Father for I have sinned, this is my first confession, these are my sins." I then confessed to the Priest that I had sinned by taking an ice cream bar out of my grandmother's freezer without permission. The Priest told me that my penance was to say the prayer of the "Our Father" five times. I exited the confessional, and I kneeled down at the altar under a six foot ceramic statue of the Virgin Mary. I looked up at the statue, bowed my head, and paid my penalty of penance.

Later that afternoon I went to my grandmother's freezer box. My grandmother lived with us in the upstairs part of the house. I contemplated whether or not to take another ice cream bar from her freezer. I weighed the cost in my mind, and decided that saying ten prayers of penance was worth the price of two more ice cream bars.

Penance vs. Christ's Blood

The "Our Father" prayer was taught by Jesus to His disciples for the purpose of instructing them how to pray for the will of God. It was never intended to be used in the religious practice of penance. Penance is a non-biblical practice used to attempt to atone for the sins that Jesus has already forgiven. It is a tool used by some religious denominations to keep a remorseful sinner in condemnation with the objective of changing his behavior. Jesus Christ calls all men to repentance, which consists of asking for forgiveness and turning away from sinful activity. However, when someone confesses their sin, Jesus is faithful and just to forgive them of all their sins, and cleanse them from all unrighteousness. *(1 John 1:9)* It was not necessary for me to conduct an act of self-abasement to show sorrow for my misdeed. All that was required of me was to ask Jesus to forgive me, make a conscious decision not to steal from my grandmother again, and make amends with her. Christ's blood is sufficient to free remorseful individuals from all guilt and condemnation. Teaching eight year old boys to pray the Our Father prayer as an act of self righteousness is contradictory to the will of God and is an attempt to debase Jesus' sacrifice. (However, teaching children to memorize scripture is the will of God.)

Lord, Teach Us to Pray

The instructions given by Jesus Christ on how and why to pray, as recorded in the gospels of Matthew and Luke, are a blue print of the will of God. (Matthew 6:9 & Luke 11:2) The sequence that Jesus Christ laid before His disciples to discern the will God through their prayers was never intended to be used in a ritualistic form. In addition, it was not intended to be a practice of reciting scripture with the hope of being heard by God depending on the quantity of the words being spoken. *Matthew 6:7 "And when you pray, do not use vain repetitions as the heathen do. For they think that they will be heard for their many words".* Jesus was instructing his disciples on what to pray for in relation to their individual lives and ministries. He gave them a sequence of concepts to pray for as they were related to the will of God.

Praying effectively can be achieved by understanding the Lord's instructions on how to pray, and by having the discipline to do so.

> In this manner, therefore, pray: Our Father in heaven, Hallowed be Your name.
>
> Matthew 6:9

It is effective to give praise and worship to God as a preliminary act before bringing your prayers and petitions before Him. Praise is an entrance into the presence of God. Worship takes you past the gates and into His courtyard. Praise and worship will also contribute to removing demonic hindrances. Angels receive power as a result of the prayers and worship coming from God's beloved. *(Daniel 10:1-13)*

> Your kingdom come. Your will be done On earth as it is in heaven.
>
> Matthew 6:10

It is effective to speak prayers in specifics, with details on how they are to be accomplished. For example; "Lord I ask you to set in place the proper people who will assist in bringing deliverance to the persecuted Christians in Sudan; I know that it is not your will for them to be starving and in slavery." "Lord, I thank you for delivering me from the affliction in my back, I ask you to straighten my spine properly, and manifest your healing promise through me." "Lord, I ask you for a job that will compliment the gifts you have deposited within me."

"It is the duty of Nations, as well as of men to owe their dependence upon the overruling power of God, to confess their sins and transgressions in humble sorrow, yet with assured hope that genuine repentance will lead to mercy and pardon: and to recognize the sublime truth, announced in the Holy Scriptures and proven by the history, that those Nations only are blessed whose God is the Lord."

Abraham Lincoln, 1863

In addition to praying specifically, it is pertinent to understand that it is God's will for our circumstances on earth to reflect the circumstances in Heaven. There is no sickness in Heaven, nor is there poverty. Wars are not permitted in Heaven, neither are any results from the Adamic fall.

It is pertinent to speak and mediate on scriptures related to the prayers that have been professed. If someone trusts that they will experience physical healing, they should confess faith through scriptures on healing.

The words of faith uttered during prayer are energy for the Angels of God to fight battles in the heavens for the purposes of the Church. It is important to note that believers should be praying for God's will to be done. Many Christians are praying for their will to be accomplished, and are contending for answers to their prayers which are outside His best for them. It is the will of God to give his children the desires of their hearts when their desires are in agreement with His will. It is essential that believers' prayers are in agreement with the will of God for their lives. If believers are praying for the purpose of satiating their flesh, they are praying apart from God's will. Therefore, their prayers are unqualified to be answered. *James 4:2-4 "You lust and do not have. You murder and covet and cannot obtain. You fight and war. Yet you do not have because you do not ask. You ask and do not receive, because you ask amiss , that you may spend it on your pleasures. Adulterers and adulteresses!*

Do you not know that friendship with the world is enmity with God? Whoever therefore wants to be a friend of the world makes himself an enemy of God."

> Give us this day our daily bread.
>
> Matthew 6:11

It is the will of God for His children to depend on Him for their daily needs, both physical and spiritual. The word of God is the bread of life, and is the meal of choice to assist believers in knowing the will of God for their lives. *John 6:33 "For the bread of God is He who comes down from heaven and gives life to the world."*

It is essential for believers in Jesus Christ to understand the importance of spending quality time studying, meditating, and becoming mature in Christ. The word of God, when confessed during prayer, will reveal the will of God for a Christian's life. There is power in the spoken word of God. When the scriptures are spoken with a pure heart they produce manifestations of God's will.

> And forgive us our debts, As we forgive our debtors.
>
> Matthew 6:12

The will of God is always for His children to be free from guilt and condemnation. Someone who comes to the Lord in prayer while harboring guilt feels unworthy to request the manifestation of the will of God in his life. When someone confesses his sins he is forgiven and declared not guilty. Jesus spoke on the importance of repentance and of being reconciled to God. These two acts allow one to enter into the Holy of Holies through the blood of Jesus Christ.

The will of God is always to forgive offenders that are remorseful, and assist those who help in the same endeavor. Jesus paid the penalty for the sins of mankind. Those who have accepted His sacrifice have been given the God-given ability to forgive others. An inability to forgive offenses is evidence that someone may not be born again. When someone is genuinely born again, God's love should be manifested through their acts of forgiveness. The character of Jesus Christ is expressed through His love and forgiveness towards those who have transgressed against the Holy Trinity. Likewise, those who have been reborn in Christ are capable of forgiving those who offend them. When a professing Christian is adamantly holding on to resentment and refusing to forgive others, he is on very dangerous ground. When someone understands what Christ did for them they have seen a perfect example of love and forgiveness. *(1 John Chapter 1)* If they accept His love and forgiveness, a behavioral response (to treat others like He has treated them) should follow. God has revealed His will through Christ, allowing them to see love and forgiveness personified. The forgiveness Christ showed others is an example to believers on how to act. The new birth reaction to being offended is to forgive and radiate Christ's character to the offender. Those who refuse to forgive may not be born again. Therefore, the benefits of salvation may not be counted to them.

> For if you forgive men their trespasses, your heavenly Father will also forgive you. But if you do not forgive men their trespasses, neither will your Father forgive your trespasses.
>
> Matthew 6:14-15

Withholding the love of God by refusing to forgive someone that offends you is sin. This is a very serious issue because it may jeopardize your relationship with God. Not repenting of the sin of unforgiveness could result in eternal separation from God. Someone can forgive an offender while still being aware of that person's faults. Forgiveness is simply ceasing to continue holding a grudge against someone and untying offense from one's heart. The act of forgiveness is beneficial for both parties involved. My personal ministry experiences have resulted in my opinion that sometimes people remain sick because they are harboring bitterness within themselves, and are refusing to forgive someone that has offended them.

> And do not lead us into temptation, but deliver us from the evil one. For Yours is the kingdom and the power and the glory forever. Amen.
>
> Matthew 6:13

God's will is that all of His children live a life of victory over sin and Satan. *(Colossians 2:15)* The petition made to God in this section of the prayer is a reminder to all believers in Christ that they are involved in spiritual warfare. *(Ephesians 6)* This spiritual warfare is being waged all around them by the heavenly and fallen Angels. *(Daniel 10:13)* The petitions of believers assist the heavenly angels in triumphing over principalities in the Heavens. Praying for the will of God makes one aware that there is a spiritual battle being waged, and makes the believer cognizant of Satan's schemes. Through calling upon ministering angels, renewing the mind, and applying the word of God, believers are counteracting the snares of Satan.

here are some professed believers in Jesus Christ within the universal body of Christ, who have spoken against His Last Will and Testament. They have outward godliness, but have never accepted Jesus genuinely as their Savior. Many of these religionists preach doctrines denying the manifestations of the will of God. They continue to wound the Holy Spirit in their actions by prohibiting Him from administering God's desires to us through divine healing, manifestations of the gifts of the Spirit, effective discipleship, impartation, and prayer. They misrepresent the will of God to appease the adherents of lukewarm religiosity. Their appeasement contributes to the defeated state that their followers live under. These professing religionist believers may not be born again; therefore, they may be qualified to be recipients of the dreadful words that will be spoken by Jesus Christ at the great white throne judgment:

> *"I never knew you; depart from Me..."*

Chapter Three

"Many will say to me in that day, 'Lord, Lord, have we not prophesied in thy name? And in thy name have cast out devils? And in thy name done many wonderful works?' "

Matthew 7:22 (KJV)

I was awakened by the sound of the door bell at 10:00 a.m. one Tuesday morning. I had worked a double shift the day before and was not completely rested. I quickly put on my workout shorts and scurried down the stairs to the front door. After getting the dogs to shut up (an impressive feat in itself), I opened the door and was greeted by an elderly lady wearing a pink dress and holding an umbrella. I noticed that she was holding a book of scripture in her hand. She handed me a pamphlet on the resurrection of Jesus Christ. I asked her, "Why are you distributing this literature this morning?" She responded, "I am assisting in spreading the truth about Jesus Christ." I inquired again, but more precisely this time, and asked, "But what has happened in your life to motivate you to spend your morning passing this literature out?" She responded, "Well, the Kingdom Hall doctrine states that only 144,000 of Jehovah's Witnesses will go to Heaven, but if you do enough of the will of God you may retain everlasting life on earth." I then asked her, "How will you know if you have done enough to earn that status? Furthermore, if you could earn your righteousness by doing good works to please God, why did Jesus have to die on the cross?" I continued, "Why do you think that the Apostle Paul wrote in *Ephesians 2:9, 'Not of works, lest any man should boast.'"* She gave me the "deer caught in the headlights" look, and then responded, "Jesus Christ is not God, and He is nothing more than the Son of God." I then asked, "Do you know the Name God used when Moses asked Him who he was to say sent him to the Hebrew people?" She responded, "No, I do not know." I then informed her that the Name God used was "I AM", and that Jesus called Himself the "I AM" as recorded in the gospels. I told her that being a witness for Jehovah required knowing who He is. She looked at me with a frustrated look on her face as she fled my front door. I realized that the spirit of false religion had deceived her into becoming incapable to receive admonishment from the word of God. However, there was a turning point for her when she made a conscious decision to fall in love with the lies that Jesus Christ is not God, and that there is not a literal Hell.

Matthew 7:22 is the Lord's rebuttal to all those who have espoused Satan's lie that one can earn God's favor with religious works. The false religions birthed through deception all hold to the doctrine of salvation through works.

Christianity teaches that it is *"Not by our works of righteousness which we have done, but according to His mercy He saved us, through the washing of regeneration, and renewing of the Holy Spirit." (Titus 3:5)*

Unfortunately there are some believers in Jesus Christ who will attempt to justify themselves by their works. They will confess before God that He is their Lord, but they will never have been regenerated by His Spirit. It is necessary to note that the Lord never states that they actually did the things that they will confess they did. I believe that out of the great multitude that will be professing their good works many will have actually done some. When someone is truly born again he will realize the times he has stepped into the flesh, instead of having proceeded in faith. The acid test is whether or not the Holy Spirit is permitted access to correct their fleshly behavior.

Casting Out Demons

Someone that is in Christ has authority to cast out demons. This authority is an indication that someone actually does know Jesus Christ. Many professed Christians that claim that they have cast out demons have not actually done so. Casting out a demon is not a drawn-out process involving holy water. Demons have to respond to the authority of an "In Christ" Christian. The book of Acts records an event that shows that those who do not know Jesus Christ will have a hard time when attempting to cast out devils. One particular demon humiliated a group of men because the men attempted to cast out the demon without knowing Jesus Christ. *Acts 19:15-16 "And the evil spirit answered and said, 'Jesus I know, and Paul I know; but who are you?' Then the man in whom the evil spirit was leaped on them, overpowered them, and prevailed against them, so that they fled out of that house naked and wounded."* They must have been beaten quite severely if they had to run out of the house naked and wounded.

The Pharisees accused Jesus of casting out devils with satanic power. (Matthew 12:27-30) Jesus reminded the Pharisees that even their own followers routinely cast out devils, and that, therefore, their notion that Jesus' casting out of demons was evil would also apply to them. I believe that many who will say that they cast out devils in the Lord's name (Yahweh) actually participated in the activity in the pre-resurrection period. The effectiveness of their activities in casting out devils is not recorded in scripture. There are different levels of power in the demonic realm. All demonic powers are under the foot of the weakest Christian; however, the followers of the Pharisees did not have that type of authority. During the period that Jesus Christ was establishing His ministry it was partly made up former members of religious groups that included (but were not limited to) the Pharisees. Many of these members probably cast out demons before Jesus Christ commenced

His ministry. During the great white throne judgment, these individuals' unsaved compatriots will be truthful in saying that they cast out devils; however, their rejection of Jesus Christ proved they never knew Him.

When studying a certain passage of scripture, it is important to read all the scriptures related to the one being studied – and it is equally important to consider the entire text and context surrounding the passage. The petrifying passage of scripture found in Matthew 7:21-23 was spoken by Jesus after He warned the multitudes of false prophets. Jesus warned of false prophets who would come from professing believers among them. He told the multitudes that they could be discerned by their fruits. Discerning the heart of an individual can be accomplished by measuring what he is producing in his ministry. The expected response to being born again is doing the will of God. The will of God being accomplished is measured through the fruits of the Spirit being manifested in the life of a believer. Many will do good works in acts of self-righteousness without ever truly being born again. The prerequisite to doing the will of God is receiving what He has done on the Cross.

> 13Enter by the narrow gate; for wide is the gate and
> broad is the way that leads to destruction, and
> there are many who go in by it. 14Because narrow
> is the gate and difficult is the way which leads
> to life, and there are few who find it. 15Beware

> of false prophets, who come to you in sheep's
> clothing, but inwardly they are ravenous wolves.
> [16]You will know them by their fruits. Do men gather
> grapes from thornbushes or figs from thistles?
> [17]Even so, every good tree bears good fruit, but
> a bad tree bears bad fruit. [18]A good tree cannot
> bear bad fruit, nor can a bad tree bear good fruit.
> [19]Every tree that does not bear good fruit is cut
> down and thrown into the fire. [20]Therefore by their
> fruits you will know them.
>
> Matthew 7:13-20

Rotten fruit is commonly found in those who are habitually self-righteous. Many supposed Christian denominations confess that Jesus Christ is Lord, but have added religious requirements to being "truly" saved. These denominations and religions possibly do not have faith that the reconciliatory work of Jesus Christ is sufficient for salvation. These religionists believe that they are required to be the convicting force that brings people into sanctification. They have usurped the Holy Spirit's job (to convict) with their own religious requirements. If someone is not living up to their standards of righteousness, they believe that the person is not saved. They preach a legalistic doctrine which prohibits their members from doing certain activities. They possibly do not have faith in the reconciliation to God that is only available through the blood of Jesus, and are easily offended when someone who confesses to know God is not convicted over something they feel is not pleasing to God. I am not referring to immorality or sins that are clearly shown as wrong in scripture. The clarity of the scriptures assists in ensuring that those who are in open sins of immorality are dealt with. (1 Corinthians 5:6-8)

One of the reasons Jesus Christ preached His Sermon on the Mount was to inform the Jews that the way they were striving to become righteous through religious works was insufficient. Jesus informed them that they would have to do much better than the Scribes and Pharisees to obtain entrance into the Kingdom of Heaven. The only way they could do better than their religious teachers was to cease from their works, and enter into Sabbath rest; and the only way they could enter into Sabbath rest was to receive the Lord of the Sabbath as their Savior.

> For the Son of Man is Lord even of the Sabbath."
>
> Matthew 12:8

The Judaizers

Many professed believers in Jesus Christ resemble the Judaizers, who insisted that a new believer had to be circumcised to be saved. The Apostle Paul was adamant in discrediting any doctrine that insisted on adding works to what Christ accomplished on the Cross.

> "Stand fast therefore in the liberty by which Christ has made us free, and do not be entangled again with a yoke of bondage. Indeed I, Paul, say to you that if you become circumcised, Christ will profit you nothing. And I testify again to every man who becomes circumcised that he is a debtor to keep the whole law. You have become estranged from Christ, you who attempt to be justified by law; you have fallen from grace. For we through the Spirit eagerly wait for the hope of righteousness by faith. For in Christ Jesus neither circumcision nor uncircumcision avails anything, but faith working through love."
>
> Galatians 5:1-6

Church Leaven

Church parishioners that do not follow religious traditions are sometimes referred to by self–righteous religious denominations as leaven. Leaven is a symbol of sin found in the Bible that has the potential to infect an entire group of believers. The leaven recorded in the Bible was a small portion of uncooked dough that was allowed to ferment. The process of time and fermentation resulted in the whole lump of dough becoming contaminated. The fermented leaven was then mixed with fresh dough, causing cross-contamination. Therefore, the new product would be useless. The debate over the necessity to be circumcised to be truly saved is not a hot topic in Christendom today. However, there are many other issues that are regularly mandated in churches that are a result of the same demonic spirit. Judging women in church who are not wearing long dresses or proclaiming that make-up is evil are unnecessary restrictions. These are only a few examples of the many legalistic demands that are placed on Christians today. The Judaizers insisted on adding circumcision to achieve righteousness, and many Christian denominations have added stipulations to the grace of God. Modesty is the will of God and should be a standard that all Christians contend for. One way to accomplish the will of God in a body of believers is to simply preach the word of God, and live an example of modesty through love. Forcing believers to follow a set a rules are attempts by churches to maintain appearances of holiness. Is it any wonder that so many new converts don't go to church? They are looked down upon and told by brainwashed religionists that if they really loved Jesus they would dress and act like them. Sanctification is a process! In fact, it is their attitude of self-righteousness that is the contaminated leaven.

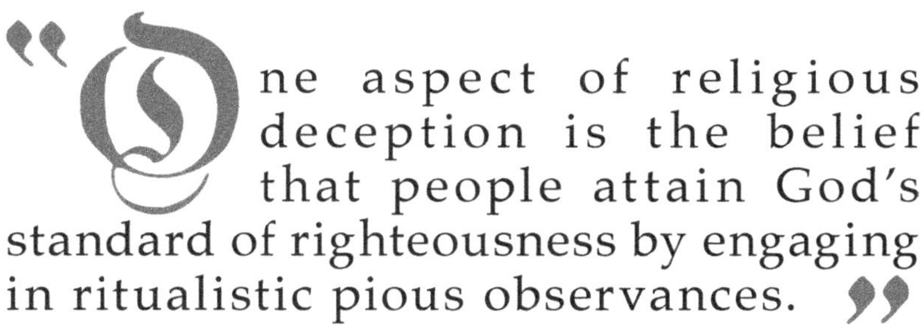

Jesus is recorded in *Matthew 5:20* as having said, *"For I say to you, that unless your righteousness exceeds the righteousness of the scribes and Pharisees, you will by no means enter the kingdom of heaven."* The scribes and Pharisees remained in their sins because they had not received the Messiah, and believed that their sanctification was based upon how well they kept the Law of Moses. Jesus explained to the hypocritical Pharisees that becoming righteous through the works of the law was unachievable. (Luke 12:1) Religious teachers that espouse the doctrine of justification through works may be qualified to be judged with the religious Jews who rejected their Messiah. The only way anyone can do better then the scribes and Pharisees is if they accept Jesus totally as God and redeemer.

> Therefore I said to you that you will die in your sins; for if you do not believe that I am He, you will die in your sins.
>
> John 8:24

The Apostle Paul exhorted the elders of the various churches that he established to rebuke those who were mixing Jewish traditions and commandments with the message of the gospel. Paul expressly labeled them as unbelieving because they refused to accept that Christ's sacrifice was sufficient to redeem them from their sin.

Paul wrote in *Titus 1:16, "They profess to know God, but in works they deny Him, being abominable, disobedient, and disqualified for every good work."* One reason they were disqualified for every good work was that they did not follow God's plan for fulfilling the will of God. The will of God is the production of the fruits of the Spirit. The only way to produce the fruits of the Spirit is through truthful spiritual understanding.

> "For this reason we also, since the day we heard it, do not cease to pray for you, and to ask that you may be filled with the knowledge of His will in all wisdom and spiritual understanding; that you may walk worthy of the Lord, fully pleasing Him, being fruitful in every good work and increasing in the knowledge of God. Strengthened with all might, according to His glorious power, for all patience and longsuffering with joy;"
>
> Colossians 1:9-11

The spiritual understandings that Paul referred to in the book of Colossians consist of, but are not limited to, the following truths:

1. The power of Christ to overcome temptations is available to all born again Christians.

2. Every born again Christian has been removed from Satan's Kingdom of darkness, and placed in Christ's Kingdom of light.

3. The blood of Jesus has released all born again Christians from Satan's bondages.

4. Jesus Christ is the exact likeness of the unseen God.

5. Born again Christians are called to serve humanity as Christ's representatives on Earth.

Those five spiritual truths are the prerequisites to being qualified to fulfill the will of God. When someone has spiritual understanding they are qualified to represent the Trinity, and their labors of love produce results pleasing to God. The fruits of righteousness help people come to know Jesus Christ and help God's laborers increase in their knowledge of Him.

The Sin of the Pepperoni Pizza

As a ten year old boy attending the local parochial school I awaited the season of lent with anticipation. The school cafeteria would serve pizza for lunch every Friday during the 40 days of lent. This was customary because eating certain types of meats on Fridays during lent is discouraged by the Roman Catholic Church. One particular Friday while I was eating my pizza during the lent season I noticed that there was pepperoni on the pizza. Usually the pizza would not include pepperoni on it, but that particular day they accidentally served it with pepperoni. I motioned for the cafeteria Nun to come over to me as I was sitting at the table and said, "Look, there is pepperoni on my pizza."

With an exasperated sigh she said, "Oh, we have to stop eating the pizza." She then proceeded to have all my fellow classmates walk over to the trash and throw out their pizza. At the age of ten, I realized that no matter how hard people tried to follow an ordinance there was always going to be a time when it would be broken unintentionally. After I had received Jesus Christ as my Savior and began to read the Bible I discovered some interesting passages written by the Apostle Paul. In the epistle Paul wrote to Timothy he prophesied that in latter days religious teachers would teach foolish doctrines, and that some of these teachings would include prohibiting people from eating certain meats, and prohibiting marriage.

> Now the Spirit expressly says that in latter times some will depart from the faith, giving heed to deceiving spirits and doctrines of demons, speaking lies in hypocrisy, having their own conscience seared with a hot iron, forbidding to marry, and commanding to abstain from foods which God created to be received with thanksgiving by those who believe and know the truth. For every creature of God is good, and nothing is to be refused if it is received with thanksgiving; for it is sanctified by the word of God and prayer.
>
> 1 Timothy 4:1-5

Many denominations that proclaim that Jesus Christ resurrected from the dead have added additional requirements and ordinances to the doctrine of grace. These denominations are adding requirements to the New Covenant in the same way that the Hebrew priests added to the Old Covenant. People who trust in their works to be freed from the penalty of their sins have either rejected God's Grace or have never been taught the significance of becoming born again. The memory of the parochial school Nuns throwing out pans of pizza that Friday during lent is not only comical, but evidence of one's inability to please God through his works.

The Sadducees

Many presumed believers in Jesus Christ resemble the Sadducees in that they deny the supernatural. The Sadducees were members of a religious order who adamantly opposed Jesus and His teachings. They did not believe in the bodily resurrection from the dead or life after death, and attempted to discredit Jesus by asking questions which exposed their own flawed theology. This particular question and the responses of Jesus are recorded in all three of the synoptic Gospels.

> Then some Sadducees-men who believed that death is the end of existence, that there is no resurrection came to Jesus with this: 'The laws of Moses state that if a man dies without children, the man's brother shall marry the widow, and their children will legally belong to the dead man, to

carry on his name. We know of a family of seven brothers. The oldest married and then died without any children. His brother married the widow and he, too, died. Still no children. And so it went, one after the other, until each of the seven had married her and died, leaving no children. Finally the woman died also. Now here is our question: Whose wife will she be in the resurrection? For all of them were married to her!'

Jesus replied, "Marriage is for people here on earth, but when those who are counted worthy of being raised from the dead get to heaven, they do not marry. And they never die again; in these respects they are like angels, and are sons of God, for they are raised up in new life from the dead. But as to your real question-whether or not there is a resurrection-why, even the writings of Moses himself prove this. For when he describes how God appeared to him in the burning bush, he speaks of God as 'the God of Abraham, the God of Isaac, and the God of Jacob.' To say that the Lord is some person's God means that person is alive, not dead!

So from God's point of view, all men are living.' 'Well said, sir!' remarked some of the experts in the Jewish law who were standing there. And that ended their questions, for they dared ask no more!" (TLB)

Luke 20:27-40

The Sadducees were notorious for attempting to discredit their opponents by coming up with half-baked hypothetical questions. Their hope was to discredit Jesus by asking Him a question they thought He could not answer. However, Jesus' wisdom was far above that of the religious Sadducees, and His response revealed them as incapable of discerning the truth of God's word. Like the Sadducees, there are professing Christians who do not believe in the supernatural manifestations of the Holy Spirit. The same demonic influence that deceived the Sadducees has infiltrated those Christian denominations. They state that manifestations of healings, tongues, interpretations, prophecies, etc. are no longer God's will. They will even go so far as to commit blasphemy towards the Holy Spirit by accrediting the supernatural to the devil. I believe that many of them have chosen to believe Satan's lies. They have not experienced the supernatural manifestations in their Christian life and as such have chosen to declare them heresies, rather than contend for them in their lives. As I have stated in the second chapter, the church age has not ended. Sometimes God's will is accomplished through the supernatural manifestations of the Holy Spirit. Unfortunately, many Christians are being instructed by teachers deceived in the area of God's will concerning supernatural manifestations. Some results of their religionist instructions are powerless Christian walks. Their Christian calling will be hindered because they have rejected the revealer. The allure to limit the manifestation of the Holy Spirit is a byproduct of lukewarm Christianity. The Devil lies to lukewarm pastors and preachers by telling them that their parishioners and visitors will be offended or uncomfortable if the Holy Spirit shows up during their services. They have sided with the Devil by unintentionally ensuring that people are comfortable in their sin rather than be convicted by the Holy Spirit. One call of the church is to assist the Holy Spirit in bringing sinners to repentance while admonishing believers to maturity. That is a difficult task to accomplish when they are more concerned with offending people rather than the Holy Spirit. How are Christians who supposedly have the Holy Spirit abiding within them able to speak negatively of those who have been given gifts from the Holy Spirit? It seems evident to me that these professed believers in Jesus Christ are simply accommodating unbelievers by attempting to discredit those that believe and practice these gifts.

The Herodians

Many professed believers in Jesus Christ resemble the Herodians by attempting to solve spiritual issues with political activism. The Herodians were influential Jews who attempted to solve secular problems by intermingling religion with politics. When Jesus was in Jerusalem the Herodians attempted to trap Jesus on the issue of paying taxes to Caesar. The Herodians' objective was to discredit

Jesus and His teachings based on the response they anticipated He would give them.

> Then the Pharisees went out and laid plans to trap him in his words. They sent their disciples to him along with the Herodians. 'Teacher,' they said, 'we know you are a man of integrity and that you teach the way of God in accordance with the truth. You aren't swayed by men, because you pay no attention to who they are. Tell us then, what is your opinion? Is it right to pay taxes to Caesar or not?' But Jesus, knowing their evil intent, said, 'You hypocrites, why are you trying to trap me? show me the coin used for paying the tax.' They brought him a denarius, and he asked them, 'Whose portrait is this? And whose inscription?' 'Caesar's,' they replied. Then he said to them, 'Give to Caesar what is Caesar's, and to God what is God's.' (NIV)
>
> Matthew 22:15-21

Many believers get sidetracked on social issues and fail to realize that the word of God is the solution to political dilemmas. Spending time evangelizing the Gospel to the unsaved world will produce the responses to the dilemmas that trouble them. In the above passage, the Herodians were attempting to solve the dilemma that the Pharisees and Sadducees had been unable to solve – the way to discredit the Messiah (Jesus). The Herodians attempted to do so through intermingling religion with politics. Jesus recognized this and, in His answer to them, He told the religious hypocrites to keep them separate. Jesus is recorded as having given a warning to His disciples, saying,

> And Jesus [repeatedly and expressly] charged and admonished them, saying, Look out; keep on your guard and beware of the leaven of the Pharisees and the leaven of Herod and the Herodians. (Amplified Bible)
>
> Mark 8:15

There are very effective Christian ministries that are doing the will of God by ensuring that the United States' tradition of Godly heritage is not dissolved. I believe that God has qualified a small remnant of Christians to contend against legislation in the courts that have an explicitly anti-Christian agenda.

Remove The Plank From Your Eye

Jesus instructed the multitudes not to judge others for sins that were equal or greater than the ones they themselves were committing, and elaborated by asking,

> And why do you look at the speck in your brother's eye, but do not consider the plank in your own eye? Or how can you say to your brother, 'Let me remove the speck from your eye'; and look, a plank is in your own eye? Hypocrite! First remove the plank from your own eye, and then you will see

> clearly to remove the speck from your brother's eye.
>
> Matthew 7:3-5

Jesus instructed the multitudes to remove the sins from their own life first so they would be able to help others. My elaboration on the passages of scripture spoken by Jesus in Matthew Chapter 7 is based on areas of my own life where I had a plank in my eye. The spirit of being judgmental was choking all of the fruits of the Spirit that were attempting to spring from my Christian walk. This spirit was chaining me to condemnation through my own conscience. I was not qualified to point out any shortcomings in others because I was blinded by pride and self-righteousness. Through the chastisement from the Holy Spirit I have discarded childish ways and have removed the sin that was so easily ensnaring me, and as a result of growing in maturity I have learned that pointing out the shortcomings of others is not the ministry God has called me to. (However, I will be held accountable for not exposing false doctrines to the church.) Many believers in Jesus Christ, despite having good intentions, behave much as I did. Unfortunately, many of them are in positions of church leadership and have been deceived through religion. I believe that they have hearts of love, but are unaware of the influence of self-righteousness in their lives. They truly do know Jesus Christ and are born again; however, they are still in error.

Fruitful Mysteries

The deceptive religionist teachers that are among God's children were planted by Satan. The spirit of deception has overtaken their consciences, and now they propagate a lukewarm Christianity. It is the responsibility of those who are in positions of leadership in the Church to teach doctrines of holiness. The necessity to assist the sheep to become vessels of honor is the responsibility of every Christian assigned a Doma gift ministry. Unfortunately, many of those who are guilty of teaching false doctrines are functioning in offices that are supposed to edify the church. Therefore, the most effective way that I can assist in admonishing the church in regards to this tentative predicament is to compare the fruits of the Spirit with the fruits of lawlessness. I have faith that this correlation will assist in admonishing the church in discerning who among them are the wolves. (All paraphrased definitions of the Greek words from Vine's Expository.)

What Tree Do You Get Your Fruit From?

Recorded in the second chapter of the book of Genesis there is a narration of the different types of trees that were in the Garden of Eden. One particular tree was called the tree of the knowledge of good and evil. Another tree was called the tree of life.

> And out of the ground made the Lord God to grow every tree that is pleasant to the sight, and good

> for food; the tree of life also in the midst of the garden, and the tree of knowledge of good and evil. (KJV)
>
> Genesis 2:9

Adam was warned not to eat from the Tree of the Knowledge of Good and Evil. If he did eat of that tree God told him that he would surely die. I believe this tree imparted, a spirit of judgmentalism, among other things to Adam and Eve and their descendants. You see the devil only told Eve part of the truth when he told her that she would be like God, knowing good and evil. When Adam and Eve ate of the forbidden tree they did become aware of good and evil like God. However, they did not have God's complete all knowing loving judgment. For this reason, the seed of judgmentalism failed to include all the knowledge of God within it. On the contrary what it did include was the demonic seed of accusing others. God's ability to judge, like God is able to judge was impossible for Adam and Eve. The natural disgust that humans have when it comes to sin failed to come with God's compassion for people who are in bondage to said sin. The spiritual poison that resulted from their disobedience passed on original sin and consequently religiosity. Within Adam's devalued seed was the "DNA" from the Tree of the Knowledge of Good and Evil. This "DNA" from the prohibited tree infected Adam and all of his offspring with the disease of judgmentalism. This sickness produces fruits of self-righteousness that become manifest when one judges others, and believes that another's sins are worse than one's own. This is one reason why I believe religion has always been a hindrance to having a true relationship with God. Many religionists distance themselves from those they believe to be ineligible to be in right-standing with God. It is interesting to note that Jesus had fellowship with those that were judged by society as abominable in the sight of God. When someone becomes born again through Christ's seed they begin to partake of the fruits that come from the Holy Spirit. The fruits that come from the Holy Spirit are birthed from the seed of love, unlike the fruits of lawlessness that are birthed from the seed of self-righteousness.

The tree of life produced twelve fruits that sustained Adam and Eve in an immortal inheritance. When they were cut off from partaking of the fruits that came from the tree of life they began to die. The tree of life is a type of Jesus Christ and the fruits that He produces. In contrast, the Tree of the Knowledge of Good and Evil represents Satan and the fruits of judgmental ism. Until the seed of Christ is planted within an individual he will continue to be infected by the poison that was derived from the Tree of the Knowledge of Good and Evil. Satan will remain that person's spiritual father and he will produce fruits of iniquity. After Jesus Christ was resurrected from the dead He sent the Holy Spirit. The Holy Spirit administers the fruits of the spirit to the sons of God. This assists those who are born again to do

Christ's work. Following the Great White Throne Judgment the full measure of God's sustaining tree of eternal life will become available once again: the Book of Revelation gives a promise that the tree of life will return. This tree will produce twelve fruits a year. One fruit will be provided each month, and the inhabitants of the New Heaven and the New Earth will partake of them.

> And he showed me a pure river of water of life, clear as crystal, proceeding out of the throne of God and of the Lamb. In the midst of the street of it, and on either side of the river, was there the tree of life, which bare twelve manner of fruits, and yielded her fruit every month: and the leaves of the tree were for the healing of the nations. And there shall be no more curse: but the throne of God and of the Lamb shall be in it; and his servants shall serve him..." (KJV)
>
> Revelation 22:1-3

Each fruit will contain a characteristic that represents God. As a result, man will be able to be nourished by the very essence of God himself. What a wonderful revelation!

Presently all those who are in Christ already have access to the tree of life: they can go to the word of God and partake of it, and the Holy Spirit is available to assist them in producing fruits of righteousness.

What Do They Do And Teach?

Discerning those who are teachers of deception can be done effectively by paying attention to what they do and teach. (Matthew 15:11) If they are producing fruits of lawlessness, rather than fruits of the Holy Spirit, they may be deceptive wolves sown by Satan. The fruit from "The Tree of The Knowledge of Good and Evil" was desirable to partake from.

> And when the woman saw that the tree was good for food, and that it was pleasant to the eyes, and a tree to be desired to make one wise, she took of the fruit thereof, and did eat, and gave also unto her husband with her; and he did eat, and the eyes of them both were opened, and they knew that they were naked; and they sewed fig leaves together, and made themselves aprons. (KJV)
>
> Genesis 3:6-7

The poison and results of disobedience were not apparent in the outward appearance of the fruit from the tree of the knowledge of good and evil. On the contrary, on the outside the fruit looked very desirable. Likewise, Satan is able to masquerade as an angel of light even though he is internally corrupt. Those who are not born again who have been sown among the wheat will appear religious and holy. Their true character will be clothed in religious works, much like the fig leaves that Adam and Eve clothed themselves with after they sinned. The Apostle Paul warned the church in Corinth that wolves like these would attempt to teach against God's will.

> But what I do, I will also continue to do, that I may cut off the opportunity from those who desire an opportunity to be regarded just as we are in the things of which they boast. For such are false apostles, deceitful workers, transforming themselves into apostles of Christ. And no wonder! For Satan himself transforms himself into an angel of light. Therefore it is no great thing if his ministers also transform themselves into ministers of righteousness, whose end will be according to their works."
>
> 2 Corinthians 11:12-15

The works they believe are assisting in their self righteousness may be the works that will seal their deportation from His presence. The angels will remove them and cast them into the lake of fire. They will be removed because they are not citizens of Heaven and have no right to remain there. They will have failed to petition for their rightful immigrant visa (green card) of redemption through the blood of Christ. As a result of not being born again on earth they will be ineligible for citizenship in Heaven. They will then try to enter heaven by attempting to climb the wall of self righteousness. Jesus clearly told mankind that those that try to enter any way other than through the Door (Himself) would be denied entry. Such people are referred to as thieves and robbers who come to steal, kill and destroy. They have the same agenda as their father the devil. These people can be recognized at times by discerning the way they police the saints, and attempt to remain in right standing with God by adherence to religious mandates. They are quick to accuse others of lawlessness just like the devil does. They may be cast into the lake of fire after the great white throne judgment. These false prophets will include those that came before and after the arrival of Jesus Christ on the earth. Discerning the spiritual condition of someone who is over you in authority, or attempting to Lord over you, can sometimes be determined by recognizing the type of fruits they produce. However, it is important to note that making a determination about someone's spiritual condition should be conducted to ensure you and/or those entrusted to you are not being deceived. Even if a spiritual leader is born again, but habitually exhibits characteristics of rotten fruit, we should be careful to ensure the leader is qualified and trustworthy to watch over us.

The fruits of faith and lawlessness, respectively, are explicitly revealed in the Bible. (Galatians 5, Proverbs 11:20, 1 Peter 1:22, Ephesians 5:9, etc.)

In the next pages we'll list and discuss some of the fruits of faith as we compare them to the fruits of lawlessness.

Fruits of Faith	Fruits of Lawlessness
Love	Wickedness
Joy	Idolatries
Peace	Murders
Patience	Thefts
Kindness	Covetousness
Goodness	Adulteries
Faithfulness	Deceitfulness
Gentleness	Licentiousness
Self Control	Jealousies
Righteousness	Blasphemy
Truth	Pride
Wisdom	Foolishness

The Fruits of the Wolves

Wickedness

Wickedness is defined by the Greek word Poneria, and it represents habitual acts of rebellion towards God's commandments. The word "wickedness" is often used to describe Satan. Professing Christians that believe grace is a credit card to live a sinful life are either incorrectly taught or their hearts have not been changed through the process of regeneration.

Idolatries

Idolatry is defined by Greek word Eidolatria, and it represents creating an image to represent a false god. Idolatry includes pagan worship and is not limited to statues, crosses, and tangible items to which people give adoration. Idolatry can be anything that takes the place of the will of God in a person's life. Many people have allowed Satan an open door into their lives with objects that take the place of a true relationship with Jesus Christ. Idolatrous outward symbols of Christianity have contributed to the replacement of the personal face to face witnessing of the born again message.

Murders

Murder is defined by Greek word Phonos, and it represents the act of taking another person's life through a variety of different acts. Though few in church have actually taken someone else's life, many are "murdering" others through the words they speak against them. If a professing Christian leader is habitually talking about the brethren in a negative light, he may be a wolf sown by Satan for the purpose of murdering the saints with His words. The important thing to note is that he may be a Wolf, that doesn't necessarily mean that he is a wolf, but that he may just be immature and unqualified in the area of love.

Thefts

Theft is defined by the Greek word Klope, and it is related to the word "kleptomaniac." It represents the act of taking something that does not belong to you through deception. Many professing Christians only attend church for the purposes of deceiving and stealing from other Christians. They may come with a business or financial opportunity, and use church contacts to peddle their agenda. The end result is sorrowful for those who trust in the scheme of the Devil to make them rich. Financial prosperity is the will of God for all His children; however, attempts to deceive the church by propagating the sole goal of gaining prosperity is outside the will of God. True prosperity is achieved within the scope of God's will through obedience to the precepts and principles presented in the scriptures. Those who are withholding the portion of their money that belongs to God (tithes) are engaging in thievery. Wolves come to steel sheep and what belongs to the Shepherd.

Covetousness

Covetousness is defined by Greek word Epithumeo, which describes the activity of desiring something or someone that belongs to another person. Jesus warned against covetousness and things that had no spiritual value. Wolves covet the Shepherd's sheep. Jesus declared in *Luke 12:15,"Take heed, and beware of covetousness: for a man's life consisteth not in the abundance of the things which he possesseth." (KJV)* Many professing Christians will lustfully desire the blessings of their fellow brothers and sisters in Christ, and they often try to take the blessings in question from such people. One example of this is when someone attempts to steal a minister's office through usurpatious rebellion. This is evidence that that individual may be a wolf in sheep's clothing. There are also professed Christian leaders who refuse to release their best people into the harvest field because they covet the contributions being made to their ministry. They do not have sufficient faith in the biblical truth stated in *Luke 6:38: "Give, and it will be given to you: good measure, pressed down, shaken together, and running over will be put into your bosom. For with the same measure that you use, it will be measured back to you."* (When Jesus stated the above quote, he was referring to the spiritual truth of the effectiveness of forgiveness. However, when you read through the rest of the Bible, you can see that this applies to almost all aspects of life.)

Adultery

Adultery is defined by the Greek word Moichao, and it describes having sexual relations with another person's spouse. However, it is not limited to that meaning. The Hebrew people where accused of committing adultery against Jehovah when they engaged in idol worship. (Ezekiel 16:15) They put their worldly desires before their relationship with God. Many professed Christians are engaged in the love of materialism, and have chosen worldly pleasures over the will of God in their lives.

Deceitfulness

Deceitfulness is defined by the Greek word Apate, and it describes actions that are conducted with the objective of giving a false impression. False impressions can include appearances along with the spoken and/or written word. Deceitful people desire to impress others by portraying a personal image that is false. Someone can appear to be affluent when they are actually in slavery to creditors. An individual can appear to be living a Godly life, but may be having an extramarital affair. Church denominations may have a doctrinal statement that says, "The Holy Spirit is invited in our service," while making every effort to exclude Him. Deceitful people will also attempt to take advantage of others. They will promise to others what they are unqualified to deliver, and leave their followers in ruin. The demonic spirits assigned to the propagation of the doctrine of salvation through works continues to deceive many people. These people will pay the ultimate price for embracing lies and rejecting the true Gospel message. Deceitfulness will yield a fruit of disgrace unto the deceiver, and a crop of disappointment to the deceived. That is why one must remember that wolves act and look just like sheep.

Licentiousness

Licentiousness is defined by the Greek word Aselgeia, and describes abominable behaviors that are conducted without restraint. It goes further than just engaging in sinful behavior in that it scorns God's will and embraces man's depravity. Licentiousness is most commonly manifested in sexual activities that show no restraint.

Jealousies

Jealousy is defined by the Greek word Zelos and describes an attitude of envy for what someone else has or is doing. This fruit of Satan is similar to covetousness and is usually the preliminary step to the manifestation of covetousness acts.

Blasphemy

Blasphemy is defined by the Greek word Blasphemeo and describes acts or verbal proclamations that denounce, defame, and otherwise show dishonor toward God. Open proclamation of using the Lord's name in vain without reference is one way in which blasphemy occurs. The unrestrained behavior being conducted by the Jews as recorded in Romans 2:23-24 is an example of blasphemy towards God. Professing Christians who live in open sin are blaspheming God. They associate themselves with the gospel of grace by their verbal profession while discrediting the message of sanctification through their behaviors. The Apostle Paul warned Timothy to avoid behavior that was impious because it would hinder the gospel message. *1 Timothy 6:1, " LET ALL who are under the yoke as bond servants esteem their own [personal] masters worthy of honor and fullest respect, so that the name of God and the teaching [about Him] may not be brought into disrepute and blasphemed."(The Amplified Bible)*

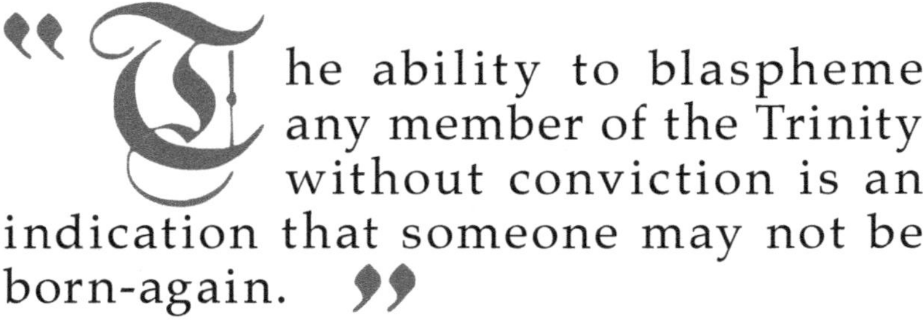

Pride

Pride is defined by the Greek word Huperephania and describes behaviors or attitudes that are conceited and arrogant. Satan fell into pride and rebelled against God's will. Many professed Christian leaders refuse to be admonished because they are prideful. Pride is manifested in acts of resentment, dishonor, and rebellion towards authority. Professing Christians who believe they have earned their righteousness through something they have done are usually partaking of the sin of pride. Many people have become prideful as a result of their accomplishments. They have rejected the God who bestowed abilities upon them and believed the lie that they have achieved success without His help. Wolves love to feel needed by others and think of themselves more highly then they are. When pride is unchecked in ministry, it will often corrupt the minister in question. These attitudes may even reveal themselves through acts of rebellion. Pride can also be manifested through attempts to discredit those in authority over them (2 Samuel 15:2-6).

Foolishness

Foolishness is defined by the Greek word Asunetos and represents activities that are conducted or beliefs that are accepted a result of a lack of discernment. An individual who denies the existence of God is defined in the book of Psalms as a fool.

> The fool hath said in his heart, There is no God.
> Psalm 53:1 (KJV)

Someone can be foolish, but may not be the type of fool who denies the existence of God. The fruit of foolishness is most commonly manifested in the church by those who insist that it is God's will for people to be sick.

It is apparent that all of the fruits that are produced as a byproduct of lawlessness resemble the character of Satan.

> The thief does not come except to steal, and to kill, and to destroy. I have come that they may have life, and that they may have it more abundantly.
> John 10:10

Discerning who the wolves in sheep's clothing are is done by recognizing what they do and say. It is important to recognize that just because a professed believer in Christ may resemble a wolf he may not actually be a wolf. If encountered, one response someone can take is to pray for the assistance of the Holy Spirit. There is a good possibility that that person is a believer who has not submitted to the process of sanctification and/or has not been instructed properly. Either way, if he is in doctrinal error you would be wise to distance yourself from him and notify your shepherd (Pastor) of your concerns. If you don't have a shepherd you need to get one!

Holy Spirit Fruits

Love

The Holy Spirit fruit of love is defined by the Greek word Agapo, and it carries the meaning of having great esteem and regard towards someone or something. It is based on grace and is not something that the subject of the love can earn. Agape love is unconditional and always places the needs of the subject before the needs of the one who is manifesting "agape" love. (Chapter 4 expounds on love in more detail)

Joy

The Holy Spirit fruit of joy is defined by the Greek word Chara and has the meaning of maintaining a positive attitude or pleasant disposition regardless of outward circumstances. When someone is made righteous through Jesus Christ the Holy Spirit produces gladness, contentment, and cheerfulness within him. The future hope of being with Jesus in Heaven produces an unspeakable joy.

Peace

The word "peace" is defined by the Greek word Eireneuo and has the meaning of inner restfulness that comes from trusting in God. Peace is also manifested through the ability to be reconciled and live in harmony with others.

Patience

Patience is defined by the Greek word Hupomone and has the meaning of abiding in faith while enduring in difficulties. The Apostle Paul used the word Hyomone when describing someone who was running a race that was set before him with endurance. The ability to deal with difficult individuals in love is an example of patience. This type of patience is referred to as longsuffering, and is described by the Greek word Makrothumea. Jesus Christ was longsuffering (Makrothumea) when He continued to love Judas Iscariot even though He knew that Judas had decided to commit treason against Him. Jesus endured the cross with longsuffering and in doing so gave Christians an example of how to love those who hate you. The spirit of longsuffering is birthed within the heart of an individual who accepts Christ, and is manifested in deed by not retaliating against someone who deserves it. One of God's chief attributes is longsuffering, as He is patiently waiting for the last unsaved person that will respond to the gospel by repenting and accepting His redemptive plan. I believe that after that event occurs the Judgment spoken of in the Book of Revelation will occur.

Kindness

The Christian fruit of kindness is defined by the Greek word Chrestotes and carries the meaning of showing honor and respect towards others. The New Testament uses the word "Chrestotes" as a way to explain the grace provided through Jesus Christ. It is through honoring all people regardless of what they have or have not done that draws people to God. All Christians have the spirit of kindness within them, and the example of Jesus to know how to treat others. Kindness can appear to be harsh when it is necessary to deny something that will condone self-destructive behavior. Kindness is shown in action when the person that places a demand on someone makes provisions to help that person fulfill the demand. Exhibiting kindness is not always popular and requires holding people accountable for their actions. It is unkind for a police officer not to issue a traffic violation if the law breaker will continue the same destructive and dangerous behavior—after all, failure to hold the violator accountable could cause harm at a later date to him or another innocent person.

Goodness

The Holy Spirit fruit of goodness is defined by the Greek word Agathos and has the meaning of being beneficial to someone or something. Goodness is the living out of the attributes of all the fruits of the spirit. Christians are called to multiply and replenish the earth through the preserving salt of the Holy Spirit that flows out of them.

Faithfulness

The Holy Spirit fruit of faithfulness is defined by the Greek word Pistos and describes traits such as dependability, trustworthiness, and perseverance. These attributes represent the characteristics of committed believers of Jesus Christ and of God Himself. God is faithful in keeping His word and covenant promises. Staying in the race regardless of the difficulty is an example of faithfulness. If someone is faithful they have attributes of trustworthiness. In addition; they are dependable, loyal and diligent in their assignments. I would rather have someone who I could depend on doing a project than a more talented person who cannot be depended upon. Someone who is faithful is willing to put the extra effort required to become skilled at the task before them. It is a lot easier to find someone with ability then it is to find someone who is faithful. A faithful person is easy to work with because he is obedient to authority and does not grumble. Choosing not to attend church on Sunday to watch a football game is faithfulness to the god of sports (but of course, this is a negative example of faithfulness). Faithfulness is a prerequisite to Godly promotion and the privilege to serve the saints as God's representative.

Gentleness

Gentleness is defined by the Greek word Epieikes and describes actions such as fairness, compassion, and benevolence. Someone who is walking in gentleness will consider all the facts of a situation before assisting in upholding the letter of the law. Choosing to put your rights aside for the betterment of another person is an act of gentleness. Jesus Christ lived out gentleness when He put His rights aside as God to live in a fleshly body like those He created. Jesus placed the betterment of humanity before His rights to deity. Gentleness is expressed in acts of mercy and pardons to the guilty.

Self-Control

The Greek word for self-control is the opposite of the Greek word Arates. Arates is a Greek word that means powerless to control oneself. Self control is manifested through having control over one's flesh. This is done with the aid of the Holy Spirit to bring the mind, will, and emotions in agreement with the regenerated spirit of man.

Righteousness

The Holy Spirit fruit of righteousness is defined by the Greek word Dikaiosune.

Dikaiosune includes within its definition the attributes of living uprightly and in accordance to the standards set by God. The keeping of this standard is only possible through the gift of grace. However, when righteousness is applied to an individual through faith in Jesus Christ they have the ability to live a sanctified life.

> For He made Him who knew no sin to be sin for us, that we might become the righteousness of God in Him.
>
> 2 Corinthians 5:21

Truth

The fruit of truth is defined by the Greek word Gnesios and describes genuineness and authenticity. Jesus Christ is the way, the truth, and the life. (John 14:6) If people are looking for truth any place other then to Jesus Christ they will not find it. Truth is what connects the Father, Son, and Holy Spirit together in complete oneness. The fruits of truthfulness should be evident in every born again Christian. The very character of truth has been implanted within them.

Wisdom

The Holy Spirit characteristic of wisdom is defined by the Greek word Sophia and is used to describe one of the characteristics of God. Wisdom is the ability to discern truth as well as having the knowledge to respond correctly to situations and people. The first act towards attaining Biblical wisdom is humbling oneself before God in reverence. The second step to attaining Biblical wisdom is being obedient to His precepts and principles.

> She is a tree of life to those who embrace her; those who lay hold of her will be blessed. (NIV)
>
> Proverbs 3:18

The wisdom of the world is contrary to the wisdom of God, and any attempt to combine them is foolish.

> For the message of the cross is foolishness to those who are perishing, but to us who are being saved it is the power of God. For it is written: 'I will destroy the wisdom of the wise, And bring to nothing the understanding of the prudent.' Where is the wise? Where is the scribe? Where is the disputer of this age? Has not God made foolish the wisdom of this world? For since, in the wisdom of God, the world through wisdom did not know God, it pleased God through the foolishness of the message preached to save those who believe. For Jews request a sign, and Greeks seek after wisdom; but we preach Christ crucified, to the Jews a stumbling block and to the Greeks foolishness, but to those who are called, both Jews and Greeks, Christ the power of God and the wisdom of God. Because the foolishness of God is wiser than men, and the weakness of God is stronger than men.
>
> 1 Corinthians 18:18-25

Christians should be producing fruits of wisdom though their lives. However, a lack of wisdom is not an indication that someone is not born again. Wisdom is a gift from God that He gives freely to those who ask Him. A portion of God's wisdom is manifested in His word, and those who seek it will find it.

The twelve Holy Spirit fruits compliment one another and are derived from the aggregate identity of the Holy Trinity. They are fruits that produce everlasting life for the recipients and benefits for those they share them with. Every born again child of God should be manifesting these fruits. The evidences of their faith are the works that are naturally produced from the seed that comes from the Spirit of God. The purpose of works is to express God's love to the unsaved, revealing the message of the cross to them. Born again Christians are not justified by their works, but their works are the manifestations of their faith in God's love towards mankind.

> 18But someone will say, “You have faith, and I have
> works.” Show me your faith without your works,
> and I will show you my faith by my works. 19You
> believe that there is one God. You do well. Even
> the demons believe — and tremble! 20But do you
> want to know, O foolish man, that faith without
> works is dead? 21Was not Abraham our father
> justified by works when he offered Isaac his son

on the altar? [22]Do you see that faith was working
together with his works, and by works faith was
made perfect? [23]And the Scripture was fulfilled
which says, "Abraham believed God, and it was
accounted to him for righteousness." And he was
called the friend of God. [24]You see then that a
man is justified by works, and not by faith only.
[25]Likewise, was not Rahab the harlot also justified
by works when she received the messengers and
sent them out another way? [26]For as the body
without the spirit is dead, so faith without works
is dead also.

James 2:18-3:1

There are some professed believers in Jesus Christ within the universal body of Jesus Christ that are actually tares sown by Satan. These tares are professing believers in Jesus Christ that have not trusted in His grace for their salvation. These supposed believers are trusting in their works to justify them as righteous in God's sight. At the great white throne judgment they will not be found in the Book of Life, and will be judged from the books listing their deeds. Some of these professed believers will have actually done good things for society, but they will have never been born again. These professed believers will have believed the lie that they had

earned righteousness through what they did. Jesus Christ warned His disciples of wolves in sheep's clothing that would infiltrate the Church. They will have masqueraded as preachers of light, when in reality they were poisoned with the fruits of lawlessness. These groups of professed believers will not have been born of the Spirit of God, and will have failed to exceed the righteousness of the Scribes and the Pharisees. As a result, these professing believers will be qualified to be recipients of the petrifying words that will be spoken by Jesus Christ at the great white throne judgment.

"I never knew you; depart from Me,..."

Chapter Four

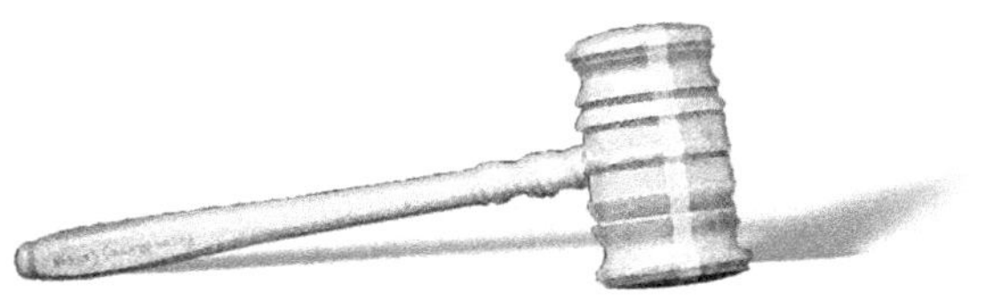

"And then will I profess unto them,
I never knew you; ..."
Matthew 7:23 (KJV)

During the first year as a Christian, I received a phone call from a television ministry that was soliciting donations. I had a spirit of pride controlling my life, and as a result, condemning responses commonly came out of my mouth. I was quick to use my "gift" with the Christian fund raiser who was fulfilling the ministry that God had called him to. After he introduced the ministry he was representing, I asked him in a loud boisterous voice, "Isn't the founder of that ministry a multi-millionaire?" He responded with a long pause and said, "I don't know, is he?" I didn't know at the time if he was or wasn't so I thought up some dollar amount in my head and said, "He's worth over 300 million dollars; why do you need my money? Go out on the street and witness to people. If my church had the money that ministry spends on television airtime we would win the whole world in a year." I then continued to voice my opinion with a condescending spirit of pride that all television ministries are ineffective for the gospel. I deemed it necessary to tell the fund raiser that the work he was doing was producing rotten fruit for the kingdom of God.

The spirits of pride and legalism had bedeviled my mind to such an extent that I was unable to walk in love towards the brethren or honor them with respect. When I look back at how immature I was during that period of my Christianity, I wonder if I was even saved. However, I know that I was born again because I was corrected by the Lord.

Days of Chastisement

The Holy Spirit re-planted me five years later in an area 2200 miles from the fellowship I was converted under. At that time I was unaware that the same television ministry that I was so opposed to was in the city I was living in. By the constraining of the Holy Spirit I found myself doing the same job as the man that I was abusive to five years earlier. Through the chastening and humor of the Lord, with the help of the Holy Spirit, my mind became renewed by the word of God. It became evident to me that the spirits of pride and legalism had been controlling my thinking patterns along with contributing to my unloving attitude towards others. I was replenished daily while working for that television ministry. I encountered brethren that walked in love, and they ministered to my wife and me when we were in dire need. I saw the fruits of that ministry manifested in the changed lives of countless people. Their efforts helped thousands of people without leaving out soul-winning. They were truly walking in love towards all people, and they revealed through their love that they knew Jesus Christ.

During the time I was working for that television ministry I was being chastened by God. This chastising was being conducted through the renewing of my mind. I routinely had encounters with brethren that showed through their love that they knew God. I am grateful that the Lord chastised me by exposing my prideful attitude of condemnation towards other believers. I realized that I was a child of God because His word states,

> My son, do not despise the chastening of the Lord, Nor be discouraged when you are rebuked by Him; For whom the Lord loves He chastens, and scourges every son whom He receives.
>
> Hebrews 12:5-6

It is interesting to note that I was not chastised by receiving a disease. The Lord convicted me in my conscience, and placed me in an environment that exposed my misconceptions. The process I was taken through was not easy on me, but it was beneficial for my sanctification. It is interesting to note that even through the process of my chastisement, the Lord blessed and corrected me simultaneously.

Knowing God Through Love

Believing that Jesus Christ is God and that He has resurrected from the dead is a prerequisite to knowing God. The evidence of knowing God is the ability to love all people as Jesus Christ did in His service and honor towards them. The will of God for every Christian is to serve and honor people through the gifts that were given to them when they became born again. The gifts given to the church are to be used in assisting the believers in fulfilling their call of ministering to others. It is difficult to both know God and walk in the fruits of ungodliness towards mankind at the same time. When the believer is walking in the fruits of the Holy Spirit he is manifesting the love of God to the world in his actions. The mature born again believer has many of the same characteristics as Jesus Christ, and resembles Him in deeds of service. Jesus Christ died so the entire world could be saved. Those who have His nature should be contending for the lost to come to repentance and be renewed by His Spirit.

> The Lord is not slack concerning His promise, as some count slackness, but is longsuffering toward us, not willing that any should perish but that all should come to repentance.
>
> 2 Peter 3:9

When someone disassociates himself from God, his ability to understand God's love is relinquished. The character of God is deposited within His children, and when it is not manifesting through them He is not properly represented in the earth. Jesus Christ has commissioned believers to subdue the earth in love with the same authority Adam had before the fall. They have been given the keys of the Kingdom of God through the word of God and their 'in Christ' authority. It is the responsibility of every believer in Jesus Christ to lay their lives down as living sacrifices to do His will. The focal point of the will of God is to minister to people and assist them in preparing to stand before Him. That is why the Apostle Paul emphasized love as more important then any gifting a Christian has been endowed with. The reason that the gifts are given to the church is so that it will use them in deeds of love towards the brethren and all humanity. These deeds of love will draw the unsaved to Jesus Christ. God is manifested in the earth simultaneously when Christians love in deed and the gospel message of salvation is being preached.

> Though I speak with the tongues of men and of angels, but have not love, I have become sounding brass or a clanging cymbal. And though I have the gift of prophecy, and understand all mysteries and all knowledge, and though I have all faith, so that I could remove mountains, but have not love, I am nothing. And though I bestow all my goods to feed the poor, and though I give my body to be burned, but have not love, it profits me nothing.
>
> 1 Corinthians 13:1-3

As Paul put it in the passage above, what good are all the gifts of the spirit if they do not assist in bringing people to the knowledge of salvation through God's love? The love of God will not be manifested if someone insists on speaking in tongues inappropriately when it could hinder an individual coming to repentance. Love is not shown in deed when prophecy is not delivered in the spirit of gentleness. When someone has a word of knowledge and abuses this Holy Spirit manifestation, the purpose of God is not fulfilled. The love of God has not been revealed when physical needs are met and spiritual needs are neglected. The love of God is manifested when someone is saved through the knowledge and acceptance of the sacrificial deed conducted on the cross of Calvary. The manifestations of the Holy Spirit are supposed to be used for the edification and exhortation of the Church. However, the only reason the Church needs to be edified and exhorted is so that the will of God can be accomplished. Jesus came to do the will of His father which consists of the redemption and reconciliation of humanity to God. Those who express God's will through works that contribute to those objectives are showing evidence that they know God. Conversely, those who are not contributing to the objectives of God's will are showing evidence that they may not know God.

The ability to understand God's love was not possible until Jesus Christ manifested love in action on the Cross 2000 years ago. Mankind was unable to love at God's standard of self denial until they saw Jesus Christ give His life for all humanity.

> Greater love hath no man than this, that a man lay down his life for his friends. (KJV)
>
> John 15:13

Before Jesus was arrested and brought before the religious council, He and Peter had the following conversation as recorded in John 13:37-38,

> "Peter asked, 'Lord, why can't I follow you now? I will lay down my life for you.' Then Jesus answered, 'Will you really lay down your life for me? I tell you the truth, before the rooster crows, you will disown me three times!'" (NIV)

Peter was confident that He loved Jesus enough to die for Him. Jesus knew that Peter was not capable of giving his life for Him at that time. That level of love is only achievable by those who know and are born of God. In the 18th Chapter of John's gospel the prophesy Jesus spoke to Peter at the last supper was fulfilled.

> You are not one of his disciples, are you?' the girl at the door asked Peter. He replied, 'I am not. (NIV)
>
> John 18:17

Peter denied knowing Jesus Christ when he stated he was not one of His disciples. He was afraid that if he admitted to knowing Jesus he would be arrested and held accountable for cutting off the ear of the High Priest's servant. Peter was willing to fight for Jesus in the Garden of Gethsemane to impress Jesus with his works. However, when Peter was separated from Jesus he did not possess the character to proclaim he knew Him. The final two denials that Peter proclaimed are recorded as follows:

> As Simon Peter stood warming himself, he was asked, 'You are not one of his disciples, are you?' He denied it, saying, 'I am not.' One of the high priest's servants, a relative of the man whose ear Peter had cut off, challenged him, 'Didn't I see you with him in the olive grove?' Again Peter denied it, and at that moment a rooster began to crow. (NIV)
>
> John 18:25-27

I have spoken to many Christians who proclaim they would not have denied Jesus Christ as Peter did outside the courtyard of the High Priest. I routinely have to remind my brethren that the new birth of salvation and power from the Holy Spirit had not been available to Peter at that time. In addition, Peter did not have an example of true love until after Jesus was crucified and resurrected from the dead. Peter remembered seeing Jesus dying gruesomely for the sins of humanity on the cross and he then understood how much God loved him. Jesus understood that Peter was not capable of laying down his life until he had seen what love was through Jesus' example. In the 20th Chapter of John, Peter and Jesus are recorded as being together once again.

The time frame of the following discussion is after the crucifixion and resurrection of Jesus.

> When they had finished eating, Jesus said to Simon Peter, 'Simon son of John, do you truly love me more than these?' 'Yes, Lord,' he said, 'you know that I love you.' Jesus said, 'Feed my lambs.' Again Jesus said, 'Simon son of John, do you truly love me?' He answered, 'Yes, Lord, you know that I love you.' Jesus said, 'Take care of my sheep.' The third time he said to him, 'Simon son of John, do you love me?' Peter was hurt because Jesus asked him the third time, 'Do you love me?' He said, 'Lord, you know all things; you know that I love you.' Jesus said, 'Feed my sheep...' (NIV)
>
> John 21:15-17:

The Power of the Spoken Word

Did you ever wonder why Jesus felt it necessary to ask Peter if he loved Him three consecutive times? While meditating on this passage of scripture it was revealed to me that Jesus was ensuring that the three denials Peter made stating he did not know Jesus would be canceled out by three confessions of faith. Peter was given an opportunity to confess his love for Jesus and become born again. Peter understood the requirement of the law when he confessed his love towards Jesus.

> 'You shall love the Lord your God with all your heart, with all your soul, and with all your mind.' This is the first and great commandment. And the

> second is like it: 'You shall love your neighbor as yourself.' On these two commandments hang all the Law and the Prophets." (NIV)
>
> Matthew 22:37-40

> "This is how we know what love is: Jesus Christ laid down his life for us. And we ought to lay down our lives for our brothers." (NIV)
>
> 1 John 3:16-17

Peter had decided to love his neighbor through will when he agreed to shepherd Jesus' flock. After Peter had truly laid his life down in service for God's will he became capable of manifesting the love of God to others. The ability to love was taught to Peter when he realized that Jesus died for him.

Peter became aware that the essence of Jesus Christ is love, and after he accepted the forgiveness Jesus offered Him, he was birthed with the God given ability to love.

> Dear friends, let us love one another, for love comes from God. Everyone who loves has been born of God and ***knows God***. Whoever does not love ***does not know God***, because God is love. This is how God showed his love among us: He sent his one and only Son into the world that we might live through him. This is love: not that we loved God, but that he loved us and sent his Son as an atoning sacrifice for our sins. Dear friends,

> since God so loved us, we also ought to love one another. No one has ever seen God; but if we love one another, God lives in us and his love is made complete in us. (NIV, Emphasis Mine)
>
> 1 John 4:7-12:

Peter had followed Jesus for three years and had divine knowledge that He was the Messiah. Regardless of all the knowledge Peter had in regards to Jesus and His Deity, he still did not know the intensity of the love of Jesus Christ for humanity. The secret of the redemptive plan of mankind, as manifested in the act of love on the part of God, was not revealed to Peter until after Jesus had resurrected from the dead. Peter truly knew Jesus after he accepted the forgiveness Jesus offered to him and he became born of God. The spirit of love was imparted to Peter as a result of his relationship with Jesus Christ. This is why people who have never accepted God's redemptive plan through faith do not know God. They are incapable of knowing God because they have never received the impartation of God's love. God's love is shown in His forgiveness of sins and reconciliation of humanity through the redemptive deed expressed on Calvary. There is no other way for humanity to know God personally.

Wolves And False Prophets Do Not Love

Wolves and false prophets do not love and care for the sheep. They are only concerned with what they can get from them. They will put their personal needs and ambitions before the welfare of the sheep every time. True love is putting the other person first every time in every situation. Jesus made it perfectly clear that the entire law is fulfilled through love. When God gave his only Son to the world for the forgiveness of sins the entire law was fulfilled. God expressed His love for all humanity through the deed of sacrificing His own son.

> A new commandment I give to you, that you love one another; as I have loved you, that you also love one another. By this all will know that you are My disciples, if you have love for one another.
>
> John 13:34-35

Recorded in the First Epistle of John chapter 2:3-6 is a passage of scripture that gives us insight on how to discern who actually knows Jesus Christ and who may not. Those who do not have evidence of the following characteristics may be qualified to hear the petrifying words, "I never knew you."

> [3]Now by this we know that we know Him, if we keep His commandments. [4]He who says, "I know Him," and does not keep His commandments, is a liar, and the truth is not in him. [5]But whoever keeps His word, truly the love of God is perfected in him. By this we know that we are in Him. [6]He who says he abides in Him ought himself also to walk just as He walked. [7]Brethren, I write no new commandment to you, but an old commandment which you have had from the beginning. The old commandment is the word which you heard from the beginning. [8]Again, a new commandment I

> write to you, which thing is true in Him and in you,
> because the darkness is passing away, and the
> true light is already shining. [9]He who says he is
> in the light, and hates his brother, is in darkness
> until now. [10]He who loves his brother abides in the
> light, and there is no cause for stumbling in him.
> [11]But he who hates his brother is in darkness and
> walks in darkness, and does not know where he
> is going, because the darkness has blinded his
> eyes. (The significance of "In Him" is explained
> in Chapter 1)
>
> 1 John 2:3-11

The only way the Ten Commandments can be kept is through love. Until someone has actually been born again, he is incapable of loving at God's standard because he does not understand what Godly love is. When someone receives Jesus Christ as their personal Lord and Savior they are given the ability to love others. Love is expressed through acts in which you place the betterment of the other person before your desires. Loving those who do not love you is the commandment that Jesus gave, but you are not commanded to like the things they do and/or stand for. On the contrary, true love desires what is best for the other party. Sometimes what is best for them is not what they desire. It is necessary to stand firm in Biblical convictions, and to pray that the person engaging in habitual sin will be restored to God's will for his life. The Apostle Paul understood that walking in God's spirit of love ensures that all of God's commandments are being fulfilled.

> [8]Owe no one anything except to love one another, for he who loves another has fulfilled the law. [9]For the commandments, "You shall not commit adultery," "You shall not murder," "You shall not steal," "You shall not bear false witness," "You shall not covet," and if there is any other commandment, are all summed up in this saying, namely, "You shall love your neighbor as yourself." [10]Love does no harm to a neighbor; therefore love is the fulfillment of the law.
>
> Romans 13:8-10

God so loved the world that He fulfilled the law through giving His only begotten Son, so that all who would receive His Son would know what love is, and know how to love others.

Loving Those Who Have Secular Authority Over You

When I was in my mid-twenties I worked in a State Prison Facility as a Correctional Officer. Prison facilities instruct their employees on how to do their job through three main avenues of instruction. These avenues consist of, but are not limited to the following:

(1) Departmental Operating Procedures.

(2) Institutional Operating Procedures

(3) Post Orders.

All three of these written policies are to be used as instructional tools to ensure the departmental objectives are followed and standards of operation are fulfilled. I was a very committed Correctional Officer and prided myself on knowing all written policies to the letter. I used to vex the supervisors because when they told me to do something that went against regulations, I was able to quote a policy from the guidelines that showed that their instructions violated institutional directives. During one of the summers that I was working at the prison there were activities that were being permitted within the prison that were violating policy. I brought the violations to the attention of both the first and second level management. They were in favor of the violations continuing because it allowed the prison to appear as if it were conducting its activities more efficiently. They then proceeded to imply that they were going to make my job difficult if I kept rocking the boat. They did not come out and say it in those exact words, but it was quite obvious to me that I was not gaining any favor with them.

I was upset about the incident that occurred with management and decided to write a complaint. I completed a report that would have gained me favor with the Director of the

Department, and possibly could have caused major problems for the management at the facility. The day I was going to submit it to the human resource officer I was called into my supervisors' office and received an apology from them. I knew that they were only doing it to gain my favor so I would not formally file my complaint. However, I walked over to the paper shredder and shredded my grievance. I knew that the grievance would cause undue hardship to the supervisors, and because they had addressed the violations of the facility through corrective actions, there was no longer a need to file the grievance. However, they had still violated my employee rights through the way they initially handled the situation. I realized that even though I had the right to insist on the grievance being addressed, that the Christ-like response was to express forgiveness through my actions. The message of love I sent them opened the door for one of the supervisors to receive Jesus Christ as his Savior. I think this event is a good example of what Jesus meant when He said, *"If you forgive the sins of any, they are forgiven them; if you retain the sins of any, they are retained." (John 20:23)* **and** *"This is My commandment, that you love one another as I have loved you." (John 15:12-13)*

Be Like Jesus And Set Your Rights Aside

Jesus Christ set His rights as God aside for the betterment of all humanity! Through that action He has shown the world how they are supposed to live in love through treating people with "agape" love. The love that God has for people is not dependant on their response to Him. That is why works-oriented religious traditions will never make Him love one person more than another.

> "Self-righteous religious traditions serve as partitions between God and Humanity. Religionists partake in them thinking they are appeasing God. However, their refusal to be placed "In Christ" prohibits them from truly knowing the essence of His character."

The word love that is used to describe God is the Greek word Agapao or Agape. It is defined as esteem that is expressed in deed towards others that reflects the nature of God. Jesus did not insist on His rights as the Son of God. When Satan tempted Jesus in the wilderness He had the power to do all Satan tempted Him to do. If Jesus would have used His power to prove to Satan that He is Deity He would have been unqualified to fulfill the law through His death. The Apostle Paul expressed that Jesus was tempted like every man, but did not sin. Jesus was tempted to insist on His rights as God. However, Jesus had temporarily given up His rightful claim to divine power for the purpose of redeeming mankind as the Son of Man. If Jesus was unable to turn the stone into bread, Satan would not have tempted

Him to do so. The act of stepping into His rightful role as God was a temptation, and Jesus could have done all the things Satan tempted Him to do. However, if Jesus had relinquished His humanity and gone along with Satan's plan, the keys of Hell and death would still belong to Satan. The new birth would not have been possible, and mankind would have no possibility of ever knowing God. (Insisting on your God-given rights should take second place to the advancement of God's will. Forgiving offenses will cover a multitude of sins, and express to humanity that the Spirit of Jesus Christ is alive in the earth.)

> 1Then Jesus, being filled with the Holy Spirit, re-
> turned from the Jordan and was led by the Spirit
> into the wilderness, 2being tempted for forty days
> by the devil. And in those days He ate nothing, and
> afterward, when they had ended, He was hungry.
> 3And the devil said to Him, "If You are the Son
> of God, command this stone to become bread."
> 4But Jesus answered him, saying, "It is written,
> 'Man shall not live by bread alone, but by every
> word of God.'" 5Then the devil, taking Him up on
> a high mountain, showed Him all the kingdoms
> of the world in a moment of time. 6And the devil
> said to Him, "All this authority I will give You, and
> their glory; for this has been delivered to me, and
> I give it to whomever I wish. 7Therefore, if You
> will worship before me, all will be Yours." 8And
> Jesus answered and said to him, "Get behind Me,

> Satan! For it is written, 'You shall worship the
> Lord your God, and Him only you shall serve.'"
> [9]Then he brought Him to Jerusalem, set Him on
> the pinnacle of the temple, and said to Him, "If
> You are the Son of God, throw Yourself down
> from here. [10]For it is written: 'He shall give His
> angels charge over you, To keep you,' [11]and,'In
> their hands they shall bear you up, Lest you dash
> your foot against a stone.'" [12]And Jesus answered
> and said to him, "It has been said, 'You shall not
> tempt the Lord your God.'" [13]Now when the devil
> had ended every temptation, he departed from
> Him until an opportune time.
>
> Luke 4:1-13

Treating Others Like Christ Treats You

Born again Christians should treat others like Christ treated and continues to treat them. For example, marital couples should be attempting to out-do one another in sacrificial deeds. Even when one spouse's actions do not reflect the nature of God, he or she should still be treated with love. The example of Christ should be manifested in their relationship. Offensive words that are directed toward an individual should not hinder acts of love towards that person. However, true love demands accountability and people should ensure that love is expressed through the deed of making people accountable. (If a crime is committed the offender needs to be held accountable for his actions.) The desired result is to bring people to repentance. The way to bring people to repentance, is to treat them well even though we may not believe they deserve it. The Apostle Paul understood this spiritual law, and expressed his knowledge of it through his letter to the Romans when he wrote, *"But God commendeth his love toward us, in that, while we were yet sinners, Christ died for us."* (KJV) Because God loved us before we even came to repentance we are supposed to love others even when they are sinning against us. Do you think Jesus ever ceased in His love for those who were responsible for His torturous death? I will remind you of the abundant words of love Jesus spoke while dying on the cross.

> Then said Jesus, "Father, forgive them; for they know not what they do..."
>
> Luke 23:34 (KJV)

Knowing God By His Spirit

God knows all born again Christians intimately. The Holy Spirit bears witness with their spirit, confirming they have a personal relationship with Him. He reveals His most intimate thoughts and aspirations to them.

> "Eye has not seen, nor ear heard, Nor have entered into the heart of man The things which God has prepared for those who love Him." But God has revealed them to us through His Spirit. For the Spirit searches all things, yes, the deep things of God. "
>
> 1 Corinthians 2:9-10

The connection that takes place between God and the spirit of a born again believer bears witness that the believer in question knows Him. The following verses written by the Apostle Paul to the church in Rome clearly emphasize that all of God's children have received the Holy Spirit, and that He is their Father.

> "For you did not receive the spirit of bondage again to fear, but you received the Spirit of adoption by whom we cry out, "Abba, Father." The Spirit Himself bears witness with our spirit that we are children of God..."
>
> Romans 8:15-16

When Christians realize that the Spirit of God is a constant reality in their lives they are freed from being controlled by religion. Furthermore, religious representatives in positions of leadership that are tyrants, wolves, and false prophets, lose control over those that know God. The ability to discern the voice of the Holy Spirit is the inward witness that someone is truly born of the Spirit of God. Jesus said,

> "My sheep hear My voice, and I know them, and they follow Me."
>
> (John 10:27)

here are professed believers in the universal body of Jesus Christ that have never been born again. The ability to love in deed has not been deposited in them by the Holy Spirit. As a result of not knowing the love of God as manifested in deed on the cross of Calvary, they are incapable of loving others. Many of these professed believers are quick to condemn people who are not living up to their standards of righteousness. They attempt to keep people in bondage through religious traditions and mandates. They believe they can gain the favor of God through their self-righteousness, and have not accepted the Biblical truth that the entire law is fulfilled through love. These professed believers in Jesus Christ may be qualified to be recipients of the dreadful words that will be spoken at the great white throne judgment.

"I never knew you: depart from Me..."

Chapter Five

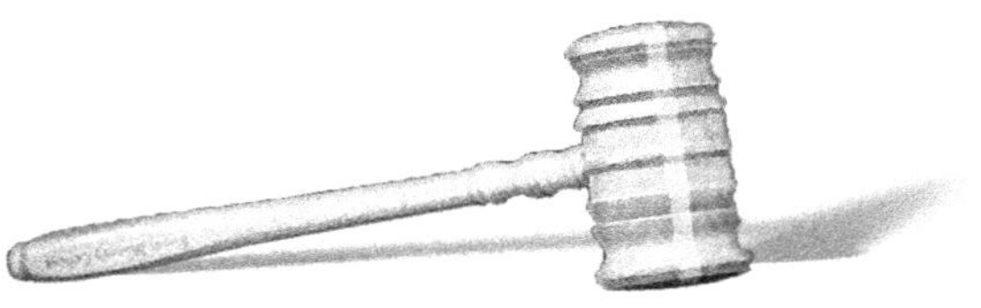

"...Depart from me, ye that work iniquity."
Matthew 7:23 (KJV)

I prayed in the Holy Spirit sporadically for approximately one week before attempting to comment on this passage of scripture. I was relentlessly asking the Holy Spirit to reveal to me what needed to be taught to the universal body of Jesus Christ from Matthew 7:23. The Holy Spirit responded with the still small voice quickened in my conscience during the early morning hours before I had awakened. The clarity of His voice with a sincere continual phrase was repeated over in my mind that morning. The Holy Spirit repeated through increments of three the following sentence: "I hate self-righteousness." After I woke up I knew that the Holy Spirit had clearly instructed me to contrast how the works of iniquity are a byproduct of self-righteousness. The exposure of the wolves and the false prophets that Jesus Christ warned about, can be done by examining their doctrines of self-righteousness. Those who practice iniquity are not only those who adamantly declare their disbelief in the gospel message, but may also be professing Christians who have never been born again. Some of these professing Christians do not know God because they have failed to truly know the character of Jesus Christ through the new birth.

Self Righteousness Is An Enemy of The Gospel

Some of the recipients of the petrifying words "I never knew you" may be professed believers that prided themselves on their attempts to please God through their religious deeds. As a result of never receiving Jesus Christ as their Savior they will be judged based on their own attempts to be righteous in God's sight. The results of attempting to be righteous through one's own efforts are futile. Self–righteous attitudes result in one being qualified to receive the penalty of sin. Self-righteousness is a byproduct of works-based salvation, and it is impossible to meet God's standard of righteousness through works.

> For by grace you have been saved through faith, and that not of yourselves; it is the gift of God, not of works, lest anyone should boast.
>
> Ephesians 2:8, 9

These people try to gain God's favor though their own actions rather than being justified though Christ. Those, who continue to partake in iniquity will be those who have never been born again. These people will have attempted to live righteously in God's sight through their own efforts. As a result of not having accepted the forgiveness for their works of iniquity, they will be accountable for them. The

Holy Trinity hates self-righteousness because it makes the sacrificial deed of Calvary non-applicable to those who attempt to justify themselves. Jesus Christ died for all of humanity and anything that hinders people from receiving the free gift of salvation grieves the Trinity. Religious self-righteousness exposes the inadequacy of man to please God. When people choose to believe the lie that what Christ did on the cross is not sufficient to redeem them from their iniquity, they will remain in constant condemnation. In addition, the hope of God's calling for their lives may not ever be revealed to them.

The following parable of the Pharisee and the Tax Collector spoken by Jesus is a powerful teaching on the importance of being justified by faith rather than acts of religious self-righteousness.

> [9]Also He spoke this parable to some who trusted in themselves that they were righteous, and despised others: [10]"Two men went up to the temple to pray, one a Pharisee and the other a tax collector. [11]The Pharisee stood and prayed thus with himself, God, I thank You that I am not like other men — extortioners, unjust, adulterers, or even as this tax collector. [12]I fast twice a week; I give tithes of all that I possess.' [13]And the tax collector, standing afar off, would not so much as raise his eyes to heaven, but beat his breast, saying, 'God, be merciful to me a sinner!' [14]I tell you, this

> man went down to his house justified rather than the other; for everyone who exalts himself will be humbled, and he who humbles himself will be exalted.
>
> Luke 18:9-14

Flamboyant expressions of religious piousness are habitually conducted by religionists that desire to receive honor from men. They desire to be thought of more highly than they are, and esteemed as individuals who truly know God. All pseudo-Christian religions have a foundation of religious self-righteousness. The denial of the authenticity of God's covenant with us is constantly preached within their circles. It is important to realize that some of those who will be accountable for their iniquity will have actually strived to please God in their efforts to be self-righteous. However, because they never were born again their best efforts will have fallen short of God's standard. The Apostle Paul wrote,

> Are we trying to pat ourselves on the back again? No, I am giving you some good ammunition! You can use this on those preachers of yours who brag about how well they look and preach but don't have true and honest hearts. You can boast about us that we, at least, are well intentioned and honest. (TLB)
>
> 2nd Cor 5:12

There will be born again people who have exercised less self-control than those who attempted to be self-righteous. However, the born again people will have had their bill of sin paid by Jesus Christ. The self-righteous will stand before God knowing that their refusal to receive the redemption through Christ's blood is the reason they will be cast out from His presence. The only way to be spared from the consequences of iniquity is through the new birth process of spiritual regeneration.

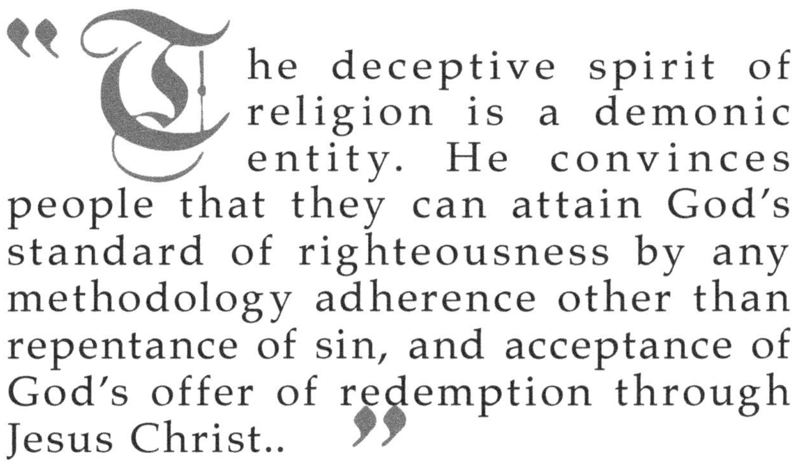

Pray for More Modern Day Judes

The New Testament epistle that was written by Jude exposed some false teachers and their characteristics. The Epistle by Jude was written towards the end of the first century A.D., and stated that the false teachers who were foretold by the Apostles were presently within the Church.

Jude said that deceivers were presently entwined within the Church and producing the fruits of ungodliness.

> For certain men have crept in unnoticed, who long ago were marked out for this condemnation, ungodly men, who turn the grace of our God into lewdness and deny the only Lord God and our Lord Jesus Christ.
>
> Jude 4

The lewdness referred to is sexual immorality without Godly conviction. Jude associated the perversions of sexual immorality with the ones that the cities of Sodom and Gomorrah were guilty of committing.

> And the angels who did not keep their proper domain, but left their own abode, He has reserved in everlasting chains under darkness for the judgment of the great day; as Sodom and Gomorrah, and the cities around them in a similar manner to these, having given themselves over to sexual immorality and gone after strange flesh, are set forth as an example, suffering the vengeance of eternal fire.
>
> Jude 6-7

These false teachers did not refuse to believe in God; however, they denied knowing Him through their habitual perverted actions. As a result of their lasciviousness they abused the grace of God and will be held accountable at the Great White Throne Judgment. The reason they believed their activities were not sinful is because they were devoid of the Holy Spirit. If they would have truly been born again they would not have been given over to reprobated minds, and would have been convicted to change their behavior.

> These are sensual persons, who cause divisions, not having the Spirit.
>
> Jude 19

The Simplicity Of Becoming Born Again

It is essential to realize that Jesus Christ is the only person who has never sinned. In Chapter Three I discussed the origin of sin and explained that it was passed on to fallen mankind through Adam's seed. This truth is expressed all through the scriptures and especially in Romans 3:23-24,

> For all have sinned and fall short of the glory of God, being justified freely by His grace through the redemption that is in Christ Jesus.

It is shown in various passages of scripture that the fallen nature of Adam was passed on to all his future descendants. Even babies are born with selfish attitudes and desires that reveal the fallen nature of humanity. God's original plan for creation did not include the now built-in iniquity of man. Adam was clothed in the glory of God and had the power to overcome temptation just like Jesus had when he was tempted by Satan.

> Therefore, just as through one man sin entered the world, and death through sin, and thus death spread to all men, because all sinned.
>
> Romans 5:12

Jesus Christ was the only one qualified to redeem mankind because He was conceived of the Holy Spirit and lived a sinless life. The penalty for Adam's disobedience had to be paid by someone. God chose to take the penalty of Adam's sin upon Himself because He did not want Adam and his descendants to go to Hell. God loved Adam and made him for fellowship. The book of Genesis records that they had conversations with one another. The good news is that Jesus Christ died for Adam and all his descendents, taking the penalty of sin upon Himself through the sacrifice of His own blood.

> For the wages of sin is death, but the gift of God is eternal life in Christ Jesus our Lord.
>
> Romans 6:23

The Rise And Fall Of Saul The Pharisee

The Apostle Paul was not one of the original disciples taught by Jesus Christ. On the contrary, the Apostle Paul was a religious Pharisee named Saul who was involved in the persecution of those who confessed Jesus Christ had risen from the dead. Paul had an encounter with Jesus Christ when he was on the road to Damascus. During this encounter Paul was told by Jesus that he was persecuting Him. This is recorded in the following passage of scripture:

> 1 Then Saul, still breathing threats and murder
> against the disciples of the Lord, went to the
> high priest 2 and asked letters from him to the
> synagogues of Damascus, so that if he found any
> who were of the Way, whether men or women,
> he might bring them bound to Jerusalem. 3 As he
> journeyed he came near Damascus, and suddenly
> a light shone around him from heaven. 4 Then he
> fell to the ground, and heard a voice saying to
> him, "Saul, Saul, why are you persecuting Me?"
> 5 And he said, "Who are You, Lord?" Then the Lord
> said, "I am Jesus, whom you are persecuting. It
> is hard for you to kick against the goads." 6 So he,
> trembling and astonished, said, "Lord, what do
> You want me to do?" Then the Lord said to him,
> "Arise and go into the city, and you will be told
> what you must do." 7 And the men who journeyed
> with him stood speechless, hearing a voice but
> seeing no one. 8 Then Saul arose from the ground,
> and when his eyes were opened he saw no one.
> But they led him by the hand and brought him into
> Damascus. 9 And he was three days without sight,
> and neither ate nor drank.
>
> Acts 9:1-9

Paul was notorious for persecuting and killing believers in Jesus Christ. It is recorded in the Book of Acts that

Paul was involved in the murder of the Deacon Stephen. It is obvious that Paul thought he was righteous based on his attempt to please God. How wrong he was, and it took a visitation from Jesus Christ to straighten him out! Paul thought that he was doing the work of God when he was persecuting the Christians of his day. The reality that he needed to be saved from his sin became obvious to him after his encounter with Jesus Christ. Paul had thought that he was pleasing God through acts of self-righteousness, and later realized that he was the chief of all sinners that needed to be saved from his failure to keep the law. Paul wrote the following passage of scripture as recorded in 1 Timothy 1:15-17,

> This is a faithful saying and worthy of all acceptance, that Christ Jesus came into the world to save sinners, of whom I am chief. However, for this reason I obtained mercy, that in me first Jesus Christ might show all longsuffering, as a pattern to those who are going to believe on Him for everlasting life. Now to the King eternal, immortal, invisible, to God who alone is wise, be honor and glory forever and ever. Amen.

Paul was not left in his sin and was given an opportunity to put his faith in Jesus Christ. Jesus Christ came to Paul when he was persecuting His own believers. Jesus did not wait for Paul to get his act together before encountering Paul on the road to Damascus. Jesus came to Paul when he was guilty of the murder and the persecution of Christians. If Jesus was willing to forgive Paul and invite him into the family of God, who would not be qualified to be saved?

> For when we were still without strength, ***in due time*** Christ died for the ungodly. For scarcely for a righteous man will one die; yet perhaps for a good man someone would even dare to die. But God demonstrates His own love toward us, in that while we were still sinners, Christ died for us." (Emphasis Mine)
>
> Romans 5:6-8

I received impartation and teaching on the previous passage of scripture that revealed to me that the world could not continue without judgment one second longer. Jesus Christ became the acceptable sacrificial goat for the sins of the world at just the right time. The judgment of the world was about to occur, and if Jesus Christ would not have stepped into the role of becoming sin at that exact second, the world would have been judged by God. Jesus Christ became the judgment of God, and if Jesus would not have been qualified to carry the judgment of the world on His shoulders, all of humanity from Adam to that present day would have been judged on their works of iniquity. This is why Jesus said,

> When a man believes in me, he does not believe in me only, but in the one who sent me. When

> he looks at me, he sees the one who sent me. I have come into the world as a light, so that no one who believes in me should stay in darkness. As for the person who hears my words but does not keep them, I do not judge him. For I did not come to judge the world, but to save it. There is a judge for the one who rejects me and does not accept my words; that very word which I spoke will condemn him at the last day. For I did not speak of my own accord, but the Father who sent me commanded me what to say and how to say it. I know that his command leads to eternal life. So whatever I say is just what the Father has told me to say. (NIV)
>
> John 12:44-50

This also is a clear indication of knowing what the will of God is through observing what Jesus said and did. Jesus did not come into the world to judge the world, but to save the world from the consequences of sin and death. Denial of the deity of Jesus Christ and the words that He spoke will be the standard to which the unsaved will be held accountable. The sin problem was solved by the redemptive deed on the cross of Calvary. God is no longer holding the sins of humanity against us. People who receive Jesus as their Savior will not be judged at the great white throne judgment; however, they will receive a judgment for the things they did in the body of Christ. Regardless of how badly, they messed it up, as long as they are born again they will not be cast out of God's presence.

Salvation Requirements

The requirements for being free from guilt and condemnation are met by receiving the free gift of salvation offered by God through His Son Jesus Christ. Someone can receive the free gift of salvation through faith in the following two ways:

1. Believe Jesus Christ was raised from the dead.

AND

2. Confess Jesus Christ as Lord and Savior *(See chapter one)*

[8]But what does it say? "The word is near you, in your mouth and in your heart" (that is, the word of faith which we preach): [9]that if you confess with your mouth the Lord Jesus and believe in your heart that God has raised Him from the dead, you will be saved. [10]For with the heart one believes unto righteousness, and with the mouth confession is made unto salvation. [11]For the Scripture says, "Whoever believes on Him will not be put to shame." [12]For there is no distinction between Jew and Greek, for the same Lord over all is rich

> to all who call upon Him. [13]For "whoever calls on the name of the Lord shall be saved."
>
> Romans 10:8-13

If you have never received Jesus Christ as your personal Lord and Savior the following is a prayer that will assist you in receiving God's free gift of salvation.

> Dear Father God in Heaven,
> I come to you in the name of your Son Jesus Christ and admit that I am a sinner. I believe in my heart and confess with my mouth that You raised Jesus Christ from the dead. I accept Jesus Christ as my Lord and Savior inviting the Holy Spirit into my life. I make a commitment to live my life for Your will. I ask you to forgive me of all my sins and I trust in the sacrifice of the blood of Jesus Christ to provide for my salvation.
> Thank you!

If you said that prayer with sincerity in your heart you are born again. Welcome to the family of God. Your salvation is assured and you are now in covenant with God. (*See chapter 2.*) You are the only one who can abandon your faith; no one can pull you from the hand of God.

> All that the Father gives Me will come to Me, and the one who comes to Me I will by no means cast out.
>
> John 6:37-38

This is encouraging in light of the study of the scriptures this book has been devoted to!

When you said the previous prayer with sincerity you became instantaneously born again in the spirit. The Spirit of God began the process of regenerating your dead spirit within you into a new living spirit connected with Him.

> That which is born of the flesh is flesh, and that which is born of the Spirit is spirit."
>
> John 3:6

Your old man has been replaced with the very essence of God.

> Therefore, if anyone is in Christ, he is a new creation; old things have passed away; behold, all things have become new.
>
> 2 Corinthian 5:17-18

You Can Overcome The Desires Of Your Flesh

The power to walk in newness of life is derived from the same resurrection power that raised Jesus Christ from the dead. The Satanic Kingdom of darkness has no claim on a born again Christian. Even though I am a born again Christian I sometimes act in ways that are contrary to the character of Jesus Christ. The decision to act a certain way or not to act a certain way is mine. If I choose to resist the temptation to sin I will have victory over it. The decision to sin or not to sin is mine to make. *"Therefore do not let sin reign in your mortal body, that you should obey it in its lusts." (Romans 6:12)* The spirit man has authority over the flesh, and will always exercise its power over it when resurrection dynamism is called upon. The born again believer has the ability to choose the road he wants to take. Before someone is born again he is controlled by his fleshly sinful desires. Many Christians still live the same way they did before they accepted Jesus Christ. These Christians do not know what is available to them through the power of the resurrection. However, they have no excuse because the Holy Spirit is continually convicting them of their sins, and has made the word of God available to teach them. Applying the word of God to temptations will produce victory over sinful desires. The decision to apply the word of God during times of temptation is the pre-deciding factor that determines spiritual victory or defeat. One tool available to all Christians to overcome sin in their lives is the option to control their thinking. The Apostle Paul understood this when he wrote the following to the Church in Corinth.

> For though we walk in the flesh, we do not war according to the flesh. 4 For the weapons of our warfare are not carnal but mighty in God for pulling down strongholds, 5 casting down arguments and every high thing that exalts itself against the knowledge of God, bringing ***every thought into***

> *captivity* to the obedience of Christ. (Emphasis mine)
>
> 2 Corinthians 10:3-5

The victory over sinful thoughts and actions is accomplished by the conscious decision to think on the character of Jesus Christ, and the power that raised Him from the dead. When you make a conscious decision to control your thinking you are resisting the Devil. The Devil has no control over your flesh. The decision that you make in your mind will determine what path you will take. The Apostle Paul learned how to be content in every situation by controlling his thoughts. Paul wrote the following instructions to the Philippians related to overcoming worry and walking in the resurrection power available to them.

> Finally, brethren, whatever things are true, whatever things are noble, whatever things are just, whatever things are pure, whatever things are lovely, whatever things are of good report, if there is any virtue and if there is anything praiseworthy — meditate on these things.
>
> Philippians 4:8

Would you agree that Jesus Christ is all the things that Paul listed in Philippians 4:8? Would you agree that you are "In Christ," and are all things that Paul listed in Philippians 4:8? I believe that if you renew your mind to the goodness of Christ that you will experience the resurrection power to live a life free from addictions. In addition, renewing your mind through the word of God is a prerequisite to being able to discern the will of God for your life.

All born again Christians have received a deposit of the very essence of Jesus Christ in their hearts.

> Who hath also sealed us, and given the earnest of the Spirit in our hearts. (KJV)
>
> 2 Corinthians 1:22

This Spirit is what places them "In Christ," and makes them heirs to all the benefits of God's covenant.

> That the blessing of Abraham might come on the Gentiles through Jesus Christ; that we might receive the promise of the Spirit through faith. (KJV)
>
> Galatians 3:14

In addition, as a result of being in Christ, they are new creatures. The creatures that they have become are spiritual clones of Jesus Christ, and everything the Word of God says about Him as a man also applies to them.

> But you are not in the flesh but in the Spirit, if indeed the Spirit of God dwells in you. Now if anyone does not have the Spirit of Christ, he is not His.
>
> Romans 8:9

Therefore, any opinions that born again Christians have about themselves that are contrary to the characteristics of Jesus Christ, are strongholds (lies) in their minds. These strongholds prevent Christians from living victorious lives, and hinders them from living out who they truly are in Christ. When Christians realize that they are Godly offspring, they will be capable of living a life that shows the world they are His children.

> For as many as are led by the Spirit of God, these are sons of God."
>
> Romans 8:14

Are You Saved? I Don't Know! Only God Knows Your Heart.

The reality is that I do not know if someone is truly born again or not. Only God and that individual know whether or not the individual has genuinely believed, accepted, and trusted in the gospel message to save him.

> For the Lord does not see as man sees; for man looks at the outward appearance, but the Lord looks at the heart.
>
> 1 Samuel 16:7

Regardless of that fact, an educated guess can be made to determine the true heart of an individual by examining the fruits that he produces. However, unless you are under my spiritual authority I have no right to try to ascertain your spiritual condition, and the only one that is qualified to judge you is God. The book of Hebrews expressly tells us that God has made known to us His laws.

> And the Holy Spirit testifies that this is so, for he has said, "This is the agreement I will make with the people of Israel, though they broke their first agreement: I will write my laws into their minds so that they will always know my will, and I will put my laws in their hearts so that they will want to obey them. And then he adds, I will never again remember their sins and lawless deeds." Now, when sins have once been forever forgiven and forgotten, there is no need to offer more sacrifices to get rid of them. (TLB)
>
> Hebrews 10:15-18

Have You Been Water Baptized?

There is scriptural evidence that many Christians do not have power to overcome sin in their lives because they have never been water baptized. Water baptism is an outward act of obedience to the word of God that publicly proclaims the faith that is inside a person. Faith without works is dead, and when someone follows through with the public act of baptism they associate their faith with a corresponding action. A spiritual event of regeneration occurs as a result of baptism in water. The 6th Chapter of the book of Romans records a revelation that Paul received from the Holy Spirit. The revelation he received was that resurrection victory over sin is manifested through applying the word of God to every sinful temptation. The word of God reveals that the act of baptism contains a spiritual phenomenon which produces power over the fallen nature of man.

> [1]Well then, shall we keep on sinning so that God can keep on showing us more and more kindness and forgiveness? [2-3]Of course not! Should we keep on sinning when we don't have to? For sin's power over us was broken when we became Christians and were baptized to become a part of Jesus Christ; through his death the power of your sinful nature was shattered. [4]Your old sin-loving nature was buried with him by baptism when he died; and when God the Father, with glorious power, brought him back to life again, you were given his wonderful new life to enjoy."
>
> Roman 6:1-4 (TLB)

I highly recommend that you read and study the book of Romans Chapter 6. It will assist you in applying resurrection power in overcoming temptations in your life.

Jesus Christ solved the sin problem for all of humanity. (2 Corinthians 5:17-18) The decision to receive the solution that he provided through the blood of the New Covenant is the choice of each individual. I do not have to emphasize to the unsaved that they are sinners. The great commission does not consist of telling people they are sinners, but that

God is no longer holding their sins against them. Those who are unsaved already know they are living in unrighteousness. If God were currently mad at humanity for their sins it would be impossible to even ask for forgiveness without personally offering a sin sacrifice. Fortunately, when a person realizes that they are lacking the way to please God they can turn to Jesus Christ and find their way into God's righteousness.

> And since, when we were his enemies, we were brought back to God by the death of his Son, what blessings he must have for us now that we are his friends and he is living within us! (TLB)
>
> Romans 5:10

People need to be told that the reason they are not right with God is because they have not entered into covenant with Him through the blood of Jesus Christ, and that His Spirit is not living within them. The blood of Jesus is the entrance into the New Covenant, and without it they cannot receive the benefits of being reconciled to God. One of the benefits of entering into the New Covenant is that their penalty for breaking the law has been paid by Jesus Christ. When people refuse to believe and accept Jesus Christ as their Savior they remain in a position of consequence. The consequence for breaking the law is death. Because they refuse to accept Jesus Christ as their Savior, their penalty for violating the law is still an indispensable obligation that must be rendered. It is unfortunate that many people will deny what Christ accomplished for them on the cross, and insist on paying the penalty of their iniquity themselves. The solution is that God has made available the opportunity for them to enter into covenant with Him through the love-deed of Calvary. However, if they refuse to enter into His New Covenant by rejecting Jesus and refusing to repent, they will remain under the law, and will be required by God to be treated as such.

> Know ye not, brethren, (for I speak to them that know the law,) how that the law hath dominion over a man as long as he liveth?
>
> Romans 7:1

> But now we are delivered from the law, that being dead wherein we were held; that we should serve in newness of spirit, and not in the oldness of the letter. (KJV)
>
> Romans 7:6

Remaining under the consequence of their sin will require them to forfeit their Christ purchased right of eternal life with God. They will personally be obligated to render the payment due for their own sins. Because they did not die to their sinful spirit man by becoming born again, they will remain in a state of spiritual separation from God for all eternity.

> For the wages of sin is death, but the gift of God is eternal life in Christ Jesus our Lord.
>
> Romans 6:23

One requirement for those who enter into the New Covenant is that they be water baptized. When new believers are submerged under water in the act of baptism, they have completed the corresponding faith action symbolizing the death of their Pre-Christ spirit man. In essence, they died to their old-selves, and have been raised to newness of life in Him.

> Buried with him in Baptism, wherein also ye are risen with him through the faith of the operation of God, who hath raised him from the dead. (KJV)
>
> Colossians 2:12

here are some professed believers in the universal body of Jesus Christ that have never been born again. The ability to cease from habitual sinning has not been deposited in them by the seed of Christ, water baptism, and/or the ability to apply the word of God to overcome temptation. They pride themselves in acts of religious self-righteousness resulting in denying the grace of God. In addition, there are false teachers in the universal body of Jesus Christ who have never been born again. They teach doctrines that are contrary to the spiritual reaction of being born again. They instruct that the grace of God is a license to engage in habitual acts of sinfulness. They insist on their rights, and cause divisions among the universal body of Jesus Christ, while advancing their perverted agenda. These professed believers in Jesus Christ may be qualified to be recipients of the petrifying words that will be spoken at the great white throne judgment.

> *"I never knew you: depart from me, ye that work iniquity."*

Conclusion

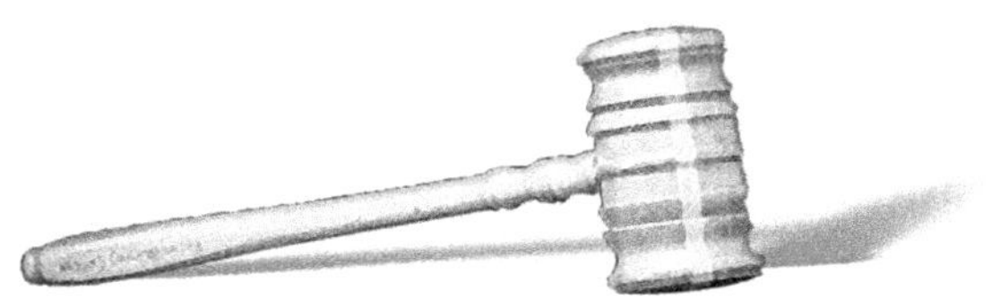

All through this book I have attempted to admonish the universal body of Jesus Christ regarding the passage of scripture that was spoken by Jesus Christ, as recorded in the gospel of Matthew 7:21-23. It is evident that those who will be qualified to be recipients of the petrifying words, "I never knew you: depart from me, you that work iniquity," (KJV) will be those who professed that they knew God and believed that they did His will through pious religious expressions. These religionists will have denied God's plan of redemption by refusing to be justified by faith in God's promised reconciliatory covenant. Those who will be judged at the great white throne judgment will come from different dispensations and religious backgrounds. Many of the religious clerics that encountered Jesus in His public ministry may be qualified partakers in this judgment. Additional partakers could be false prophets and wolves in sheep's clothing, having infiltrated the universal body of Jesus Christ. The common factor, linking these people together will be their unbelief in God's promise of justification through faith. Some of them will deny the message of redemptive truth openly while others will secretly despise it. There will be some supposed believers who will state that they had been born again. However, they will have blasphemed the doctrine of grace through acts of lewdness. The character of these professed believers in God will have been exposed by the fruits that they produced. Finally, there will be a portion of self-professed Christians that will have denied the Holy Trinity and will have attempted to gain God's favor through self-righteous acts. All those that will be partakers of this dreadful judgment are capable of having some characteristics of each group mentioned. Their characteristics may spill over into each other's groups but they may not be directly associated with one another.

My Lord and Savior Jesus Christ gave clear instructions on how to ensure that you will not be a partaker in the consequences He mentions in Matthew 7: 21-23. Immediately after Jesus warned of the judgment that would come upon religionists, wolves and false prophets, he gives the following instructions:

> "[24]*Therefore whoever hears these sayings of Mine, and does them, I will liken him to a wise man who built his house on the rock:* [25]*and the rain descended, the floods came, and the winds blew and beat on that house; and it did not fall, for it was founded on the rock.* [26]*But everyone who hears these sayings of Mine, and does not do them, will be like a foolish man who built his house on the sand:* [27]*and the rain descended, the*

floods came, and the winds blew and beat on that house; and it fell. And great was its fall."

Matthew 7:24-27

Jesus Christ is the Chief Cornerstone

Behold, I lay in Zion a chief cornerstone, elect, precious, and he who believes on Him will by no means be put to shame.

1 Peter 2:6

About the Author

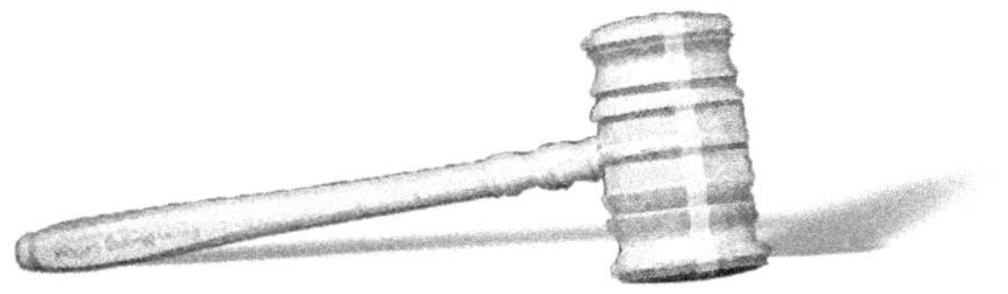

Reverend David Wlazlak has worked in law enforcement for the last 14 years in both Officer and Managerial roles. He is presently serving in a ministerial law enforcement position. David received the status of Ordained Minister with "Faith Christian Fellowship International" in October of 2007. David faithfully preaches the message of reconciliation in churches in Mexico and the United States. David's calling began to manifest in service and opportunities to minister when he committed to attend "Faith Ministry Training Institute" in 2006. David graduated from "F.M.T.I." in 2008. He has previously spent a year working for an international television ministry. David has written another book, "The Watchman's Plea," which is used to help Christians introduce Jesus to those who do not know Him. As a law enforcement Officer and Minister in a border town in southern Arizona, he encounters a good daily dose of law breakers and others who have fallen from the Lord or have never found Him. This unique experience as a combined Law/Preacher evangelist appears to have prepared him well for the task at hand. Wlazlak is known to lovingly speak about uncomfortable, seldom talked-about truths, and sugar-coating is not his trademark.

www.ingramcontent.com/pod-product-compliance
Lightning Source LLC
LaVergne TN
LVHW011231080426
835509LV00005B/430

* 9 7 8 0 6 1 5 1 9 8 2 9 3 *